DEFI:

DECENTRALIZED FINANCE

Table of Contents

Introduction

Y ou've probably heard of DeFi finance, in this book we'll go through all the steps together to understand what it is, what it's for, and how to make the most of it.

The emergence of this type of finance is due to our history, before, we exchanged goods and services, but the economy has evolved, different levels of it were created. Some currencies have had more confidence than others, but all have been centralized which makes them more vulnerable to devaluations. But with DeFi is developed as a base to have an open financial system and with the purpose of not having a central authority.

DeFi is an entire ecosystem of applications and working protocols that deliver value to millions of users. More than $30 billion is locked up in DeFi ecosystems. Therefore, they are a high-growth segment.

DeFi is growing rapidly, it has many important real-world use cases. It includes decentralized exchanges, lending platforms, forecasting, and so on. Inside, you'll find geographically unlimited access to financial services, making use of the benefits of cryptos, smart contracts, and blockchain technology.

Here you will find out why DeFi services are a great advantage to start investing. The notion of DeFi as an alternative financial model is only made possible by relatively recent innovations such as the Internet, cryptography, and blockchain. These tools enable programmers to collectively build an entirely new financial ecosystem from scratch without the need for central authorities.

As you read this book, you're going to learn all about the current, centralized financial system as well. After all, if you don't know how the current system works (or doesn't work), how can you understand why decentralized finance (DeFi) is such a big deal? I've minimized the complex jargon and presented all material in easily understandable language, so don't worry about all of this flying over your head.

This book will discuss with you everything you need to know about DeFi. It will teach you how the system works, why it works the way it does, and what lies ahead for it.

The DeFi mentality is pretty simple. Banks and other financial institutions provide a whole host of services, from wealth storage, loans, facilitating transactions, etc. DeFi aims to replace these services one by one with a crypto alternative (each service having its cryptocurrency).

DeFi aims to create financial products that don't rely on gambling in the crypto exchanges with one coin or another. It treats cryptocurrency as real money and is as serious in the business of money as the traditional banking sector is. People are already earning reasonable interest rates safely in many other ways mentioned before using stable coins. Cryptocurrencies and DeFi are taking away the services that the financial sector used to have a monopoly. One of these services is certificates of deposit (sometimes known as time deposits), and it is this service that Hex is the first crypto alternative. Let's get started.

CHAPERT 1:

The History of DeFi and How It Started

What Is Decentralized Finance?

D ecentralized finance or DeFi as it is abbreviated, is a term used for a number of applications and projects that are developed on a blockchain impacting traditional finance. DeFi are peer-to-peer applications developed on blockchain networks and decentralized refers to not requiring access rights to facilitate loans, oracles (oracles), cryptocurrencies, swaps, derivatives, and other financial tools.

The emergence of this type of finance is due to our history, before, we exchanged goods and services, but the economy has evolved, different levels of it were created. Some currencies have had more confidence than others, but all have been centralized which makes them more vulnerable to devaluations. But with DeFi is developed as a base to have an open financial system and with the purpose of not having a central authority.

In terms of the future of this type of technology, we have seen a quantum leap in the way people invest. It is difficult to predict how this space will be configured when the power to create financial services is democratized. But looking empirically, every day there is more trust and more people are betting on making a profit.

If you want to buy shares of company stock, for example, you use a stock exchange to find a seller who provides the shares at a price you're willing to pay. Most likely, you're making the transaction from an online trading platform and paying a commission to do so. Your payment compensates the platform for its role in the purchase you're making. Most transactions involving money use intermediaries or middlemen, who take some payment for their involvement.

The electronic trading platforms are, believe it or not, a step above the 20th Century way of investing in the market. Before the Internet, you would have to have a broker who you would call to do the trade. Those commissions were much higher even than the ones you pay to modern trading platforms.

Intermediaries make transactions potentially more expensive than they need to be. It also introduces gatekeepers to some of the markets, so if you want to buy into a hedge fund or private equity firm you need to have a certain net worth and income to do so.

In the type of centralized financial world that we mostly have now, central banks are key to the economies of major developed countries. Here, in the US, the central bank is known as the Federal Reserve (the Fed). It can raise or lower interest rates to pump more money in, or take money out which it typically does if inflation is running high—more about this later in the book.

If the Fed raises the interest rate at which it lends money, then all the lending institutions must raise their interest rates too, otherwise, they'll be unprofitable. The banks act as intermediaries for the loans.

Suppose you want to take out a mortgage so you can buy a house. Once the Fed raises rates (or "tightens" them), the bank will raise the interest rate for mortgages too and take a cut for making the loan.

Intermediaries employ a lot of people, which means they need to make a certain amount of profit to stay in business. Typically, the person who sells you a mortgage is not the same person who underwrites it (decides how risky you are and how high your interest rate should be), even though they work for the same institution.

Each lender has its own policies about writing loans, such as what credit score a borrower needs to have, and other conditions of the loan. You might qualify for a mortgage at one bank and not at another, or face a higher interest rate at one company compared to the other one just down the road. In addition, you'll pay a variety of fees associated with the mortgage loan (or any loan).

At this point you might be asking yourself, why do we need intermediaries in the first place, since they cost so much? When money is involved, so is trust. Intermediaries are neutral third parties in a transaction that don't have a stake in the outcome.

In the old days, companies would issue actual share certificates for their stock. Suppose you agreed with a seller that you'd buy 10 shares of, say, the American Amalgamated Agency Association (AAAA).

What happens if you send the seller your money and they never send you the certificates? You can't prove that you own the shares, and so you can't profit by selling them once the share price reaches a new high. Conversely, suppose the seller sent you the certificates and you never ponied up the money. Now the seller has no shares, so they can't sell to someone who will pay them, and no money.

The easiest way to solve this particular kind of problem is an intermediary, in this case, a clearinghouse. The seller sends the certificates to the clearinghouse, which keeps track of the owner of the shares, for a fee. Then, when you buy them, the clearinghouse notes that you're the new owner of those shares. You pay them the seller's price, plus a fee for the clearinghouse. After the house takes its cut, it passes the remainder to the seller.

Companies don't issue stock certificates anymore and the records are all electronic, but the steps are the same. The middleman or intermediary takes their cut either way.

History of DeFi

There is no singular event marking the start of the DeFi movement. Admittedly, the origins of the DeFi movement can be described as rather obscure. The term "DeFi" is best treated as a term that arose given the need to classify and label the emergence of a new type of cryptocurrency project. In this chapter, we will examine the early uses of the term "DeFi," as well as some early DeFi projects in the period between 2016 and 2018.

Early DeFi projects were mainly asset-backed lending protocols. While the term "lending" would often appear in the description of such projects, as well as numerous other projects in the DeFi space, it does not resemble a traditional "loan" agreement. A "loan," as understood conventionally, is a transaction in which one person gives money to another person who promises to pay it back later, usually with interest. There is always a lender, who offers the credit, and the borrower, who gets into debt.

Asset-backed lending protocols, on the other hand, function somewhat differently. A borrower will begin by depositing crypto assets (typically Ether or Bitcoin) and receive a loan that comes with interest. The amount which can be loaned will depend on the collateralization ratio.

From the general description of asset-backed lending protocols above, it can be surmised that such protocols function based on two key mechanics: over-collateralization and liquidation. A user who deposits his crypto assets will only be able to "loan" a percentage of its value in cash. In other words, all of such "loans" are overcollateralized since the collateralization ratio will never be close to, let alone fall below, 100%. It differs from a traditional loan since, technically, no credit is extended to the borrower. This brings us to the next point: liquidation. When the collateralization ratio falls to a pre-determined point, such as 110% for example, due to a substantial drop in the price of the collateralized crypto-asset relative to USD, the entirety of the user's collateral will be liquidated. Even at the point of liquidation, the "loan" remains overcollateralized. This would seem particularly onerous for the borrower. Throughout this entire process, the lender will, at no point in time, suffer a loss of funds or even come close to doing so. Therefore, to label such

DeFi projects as offering "loans" would come across as misleading to those unaware of the intricacies of such products and services.

In the remaining part of this section, we will examine some early DeFi projects, namely: SALT, NEXO, and ETHLend.

- Secured Automated Lending Technology, abbreviated as SALT, is an asset-backed lending protocol created in 2016. SALT offers a loan period of 3 to 12 months and the interest rate, which varies from 15 to 22%, will depend on the Loan-to-Value (LTV) ratio. A borrower's assets will be liquidated when the LTV ratio reaches 90.91%. Lenders are manually matched to borrowers and this is typically expected to be a lengthy process. The native SALT token can be used for discounted interest rates as well as repayment.

- NEXO, which was founded in 2018, is a provider of cryptocurrency-backed loans. Similar to SALT, it has a native token that can also be used for collateral and repayment. NEXO token holders are also entitled to interest rate discounts and other benefits. The loan approval process on NEXO is fully automated, without the need to manually match lenders and borrowers.

- ETHLend is a dDapp protocol created in 2017 which offers peer-to-peer loans via Smart Contracts. However,

ETHLend only transacts in ERC20 tokens. This means that loans cannot be made in fiat. Borrowers may, however, still withdraw ERC20-based stablecoins such as Tether from the platform. ETHLend offers a greater degree of flexibility since loan details can be negotiated between lenders and borrowers. However, similar to SALT, this matching process is expected to be lengthy.

Despite being the pioneers and first-movers of the DeFi movement, the trajectory of these early DeFi projects vastly differed from each other.

Among the 3 early DeFi projects, SALT presents the greatest case for concern. SALT was investigated by the U.S. Securities and Exchange Commission (SEC) in February 2018 for its $50 million initial coin offering (ICO) held in late 2017. In February 2019, SALT was delisted from Binance. Presently, SALT has a market capitalization of approximately $6 million, placing it outside of the top 400 cryptocurrencies by market capitalization. The value of its token has fallen by approximately 99% from its all-time high in Dec 2017.

NEXO, as compared to SALT, has fared much better. NEXO has provided more than $500 million of loans in USDT and USDC and has rebranded itself as a provider of "Instant Crypto Credit Lines." However, the increased centralization of the NEXO ecosystem has moved NEXO away from a "DeFi" project and towards that of a fintech or digital bank startup. While elements of the DeFi movement were present in its origins, the development of its platform and ecosystem does not fully conform to a decentralized project in the DeFi sense. NEXO is not recognized as a DeFi token by Coingecko. Lastly, ETHLend ceased operation in January 2020. Interestingly, it was not the end of the road for ETHLend since it provided the basis for another subsequent project: Aave Protocol. Stani Kulechov, the CEO of ETHLend, went on to create the Aave Protocol alongside his original team. Aave has recently emerged as the largest DeFi lending platform. We will explore Aave in greater detail in the subsequent chapter. The growth of DeFi within the past two years has been nothing short of phenomenal. The total value locked in DeFi has increased from just above $300 million in Jan 2019 to $9 billion in September 2020. The DeFi ecosystem has also evolved and matured. While lending protocols still dominate the largest share of value and attention, other categories of DeFi projects have gradually come to the fore.

Main DeFi Categories

Stablecoins

Cryptocurrency prices are well known for being highly volatile. Cryptocurrencies often experience intraday swings of more than 10%. Stablecoins—which are indexed to other stable assets like the US dollar—were designed to help reduce this uncertainty.

Tether (USDT) was the first centralized stablecoin to be released. Each USDT is said to be supported by a dollar in the issuer's bank account. One significant disadvantage of USDT is that users must trust that the USD reserves are completely collateralized and exist.

Decentralized stablecoins aim to address the issue of trust. Decentralized stablecoins are generated using an over-collateralization process, run entirely on decentralized ledgers, are regulated by decentralized autonomous organizations, and anybody can audit their reserves.

Stablecoins, while not technically a financial program, are critical in making DeFi applications more available to all by providing a stable store of value.

Borrowing and Lending

Traditional financial services demand that customers have bank accounts to access their services, which 1.7 billion people lack. Borrowing from banks is subject to additional conditions, such as having a decent credit score and ample collateral to persuade banks that you are creditworthy and capable of repaying a loan.

This obstacle is removed with decentralized lending and borrowing, allowing everyone to use their digital assets as collateral to access loans. Contributing to lending pools and receiving interest on these assets can equally earn a return on assets and allow one to engage in the lending market. There is little need for a bank account or a credit check with decentralized lending and borrowing.

Exchanges

Coinbase and Binance that you can use to convert one crypto to another. These are centralized markets, which means they act as both middlemen and custodians for the assets exchanged. Users of these exchanges have no power over their funds, placing them at risk if the exchanges are compromised and unable to meet their obligations.

Users can trade cryptos without giving up ownership of their coins on decentralized exchanges, which aims to address this issue. People do not have to trust centralized exchanges to remain afloat because they do not store any funds.

Derivatives

A derivative is a contract that derives its value from some other underlying commodity, such as stocks, products, currencies, indices, bonds, or interest rates.

Traders may use derivatives to hedge their positions and reduce risk in specific trades. Assume you're a glove maker who wants to protect yourself from a sudden rise in rubber prices. You can purchase a futures contract from your supplier to have a certain quantity of rubber delivered at a specific future delivery date for a predetermined price today.

Contracts for derivatives are often exchanged on centralized networks. Decentralized derivatives markets are being built on DeFi networks. Later in this book, we'll go through this in greater depth.

Fund Management

The practice of monitoring your assets and controlling their cash flow to produce a return on your investments is known as fund management. Active and passive fund management are the two primary forms of fund management. A management team makes investment decisions to match a specific index, such as the S&P500, in active fund management. There is no management team in place for passive fund management, but it is intended to replicate a specific index's performance strongly.

Many DeFi initiatives have begun to provide decentralized passive fund management. Users can easily monitor how their funds are handled and determine the cost they would pay, thanks to DeFi's openness.

Lottery

Innovative and disruptive financial applications will arise as DeFi evolves, democratizing access and eliminating intermediaries. Adding a DeFi twist to lotteries allows the pooled capital to be transferred to a smart contract on the Ethereum network.

DeFi's functionality allows you to link a basic lottery DApp to another DeFi DApp to build something more valuable. DeFi DApps allows users to pool their capital. The pooled capital is then invested in a DeFi lending DApp, with interest received and distributed to a random winner at regular intervals. After the winner is selected, all lottery ticket purchasers receive a refund, making sure that no one loses money.

Payments

One of crypto's most essential functions is to enable decentralized and trustless value transfer between 2 entities. As DeFi becomes more popular, more innovative payment methods are being developed and tested.

Certain DeFi project seeks to shift the way we think about payments by repurposing payments as streams rather than traditional transactions. The ability to provide payments as streams opens up a slew of new possibilities for money. Consider "pay-as-you-use," but on a much smaller scale and with greater precision. The nascence of DeFi, as well as the pace of progress, would certainly bring new ways of thinking about how payments function, addressing many of the existing financial system's flaws.

Insurance

Insurance is a risk management policy whereby a person receives financial cover or compensation from an insurance provider in a catastrophic event. People also buy insurance for their automobiles, homes, health, and lives. Is there, however, decentralized DeFi insurance?

CHAPERT 2:

Comparison Between DeFi and Normal Finance

To shed light on people who are new to DeFi, we will first go over the fundamentals of how traditional financial institutions work. For the sake of simplicity, we will concentrate on the most leveraged institutions in the traditional financial system, banks, and discuss their key areas to identify potential risks.

The Banks

Banks are the behemoths of the financial sector, processing payments, collecting deposits, and extending credit to people, companies, other financial organizations, and even governments. They are so enormous that the combined market capitalization of the world's top 10 banks exceeds $2 trillion. On the other hand, the total market capitalization of the entire cryptocurrency market was valued at around $200 billion on December 31, 2019.

Banks are vital parts of the financial industry's moving machine, enabling money to travel across the globe via value transfer services (deposit, withdrawal, transfers), extending credit lines (loans), and more. On the other hand, banks are managed by humans and governed by policies that are vulnerable to human-related risks like mismanagement and corruption.

The 2008 global financial crisis exemplified excessive risk-taking by banks, and governments were forced to bail out the banks in massive amounts. The crisis exposed the traditional financial system's flaws and highlighted the need for it to improve.

DeFi aims to create a better financial landscape enabled by the internet and blockchain technology, focusing on 3 key segments of the banking system:

1. **Payment and clearance system.** If you've ever tried to send money to someone or a business in another country, you know how inconvenient it can be—remittances involving banks all over the world typically take a few working days to complete and come with several fees. There may be issues with documentation, anti-money laundering compliance, privacy concerns, and other factors to make matters worse.

For example, suppose you live in the United States and want to send $1,000 from your bank account in the United States to a friend's bank account in Australia. In that case, you will typically incur 3 fees: the exchange rate from your bank, the international wire outbound fee, and the international wire inbound fee. Furthermore, depending on the recipient's bank's location, the recipient will receive the money in a few working days.

The cryptocurrency that powers the DeFi movement allows you to avoid intermediaries who take the lion's share of the profits from these transfers. It is also likely to be faster—your transfers will be processed with no questions asked and at a lower fee than banks. Transferring cryptocurrencies to any account in the world, for example, would take anywhere from 15 seconds to 5 minutes, depending on several factors, plus a small fee (e.g., $0.02 on Ethereum).

2. **Accessibility.** Chances are, if you're reading this book, you're banked and have access to financial services provided by banks, such as opening a savings account, taking out a loan, investing, and so on. However, many more people are less fortunate and lack access to even the most basic savings account.

According to the World Bank, as of 2017, 1.7 billion individuals lacked access to financial services, with more than half of them living in developing nations. They are mostly from low-income families, and their main reasons for not having a bank account are poverty, geography, and lack of trust.

Access to banking is difficult for the 1.7 billion unbanked, but DeFi has the potential to make it easier. In contrast to lengthy verification processes, accessing DeFi DApps only requires a mobile phone and internet access. According to the World Bank, two-thirds of the 1.7 billion unbanked have access to mobile phones, and DeFi DApps, rather than traditional banks, can be their gateway to accessing financial products.

DeFi is a movement that advocates for borderless, censorship-free, and easily accessible financial products for all. DeFi protocols are non-discriminatory and level the playing field for all.

3. **Centralization and transparency.** Traditional, regulated financial organizations such as banks, which comply with government rules and regulations, are without a doubt among the safest locations to keep the money. They are not without flaws, however, and even large banks can fail. Both Washington Mutual, which had

over \$188 billion in deposits, and Lehman Brothers, which had \$639 billion in assets, failed in 2008. Over 500 bank failures have been reported in the United States alone.

Banks are one of the financial system's centralized points of failure; the failure of Lehman Brothers sparked the beginning of the financial crisis of 2008. Given recent instances, the concentration of power and cash in the hands of banks is risky.

Transparency is also related to this; regular investors cannot fully understand what financial institutions do. Credit rating agencies awarding AAA ratings (best and safest investments) to high-risk mortgage-backed securities was one of the factors that precipitated the 2008 financial crisis

With DeFi, things will be different. DeFi protocols built on public blockchains like Ethereum are mostly open-sourced for auditing and transparency. They typically have decentralized governing organizations to ensure that everyone is aware of what is going on and that no bad actors can make bad decisions independently.

DeFi protocols are written as lines of code—you can't cheat the codes because they treat all participants equally and without discrimination. Because the codes are available to public scrutiny, they operate precisely how they are intended to. Any weaknesses are immediately discovered. At the end of the day, DeFi's greatest strength is its ability to bypass intermediaries and operate without censorship.

The existing banking system is plagued by friction, inaccessibility, and regulatory uncertainty, to name a few key problems. Unfortunately, not everyone in today's financial system has access to banking, making it impossible for the unbanked to compete on an equal footing.

The DeFi movement aims to close these gaps and make finance available to everyone without censorship. In short, DeFi opens up a world of possibilities by allowing users to access various financial instruments regardless of race, religion, age, nationality, or geography. When comparing traditional and decentralized financial products, there will be advantages and disadvantages on both sides. In this book, we'll take you through the ideas and potential of decentralized finance so you can put them to work solving real-world issues.

Will DeFi Replace Traditional Banks?

In the foreseeable future, this is unlikely to occur. While DeFi can provide many of the financial services which are typically associated with traditional retail banks, it still has a long way to go in displacing its long-entrenched dominance. In other words, the mainstream adoption of DeFi remains a distant goal.

Traditional finance is a system based on trust. More specifically, it is the trust in institutions, governments, regulators, and other key financial players which the ordinary person has that has enabled these traditional banks to entrench themselves in our economic lives. To the ordinary person, the fact that traditional banks are regulated while DeFi projects are largely not is a sufficiently convincing reason to maintain the status quo. Regulation implies adherence to standards and rules, which increases legitimacy and trust. Unless this trust in the traditional financial system breaks down, most people will not see the need for "trustless" financial products and services like DeFi. In the absence of any major disruption to the traditional financial system, it is unlikely that DeFi will gain significant traction among the general population.

The key challenge facing DeFi adoption, as well as cryptocurrency adoption in general, is the steep learning curve inherent in this new technology. For those who are only familiar with traditional banks and their services, the transition to DeFi will not be seamless. Individuals will have to learn about an entirely new financial ecosystem, as well as how basic financial products and services operate on DeFi platforms. If young and educated digital natives find this a challenging task, then it is certainly a tall order to expect the general population to make the switch anytime soon.

Cryptocurrency adoption is a necessary condition for DeFi adoption. If one is unfamiliar with cryptocurrencies as an asset class, then it would be unrealistic to expect them to be receptive to financial products and services based on cryptocurrencies. With cryptocurrency adoption still a work in progress, it would seem premature to discuss DeFi adoption.

DeFi Will Certainly Cause More Financial and Technological Innovation

With more and more entrepreneurs coming into the DeFi space, and more financial products and sectors being worked on from the angle of DeFi projects, it is certain that more innovations will occur in the space, and may result in challenges to the existing world order in the financial industry.

Looking at the still relatively low market capitalization in the DeFi space, the industry boom will still probably last for the next 6 to 12 months, and possibly mature to a certain extent in mid to late 2021, where some of the bigger and better projects will start to pull away from the crowd and consolidate their position in the DeFi space.

With the coming of Central Bank Digital Currencies (CBDCs) in the near future, it is also highly likely that top DeFi projects will be able to integrate with and co-exist with CBDCs and sovereign coins. The technology and finance sectors will integrate even more, and some iterations of FinTech will start to become global giants and outperform the traditional giants of the financial markets.

Governments and Central Banks will start to adopt a more open stance towards DeFi and Fintech and also become more digital in their nature and approach to monetary and fiscal policies.

There may also finally be some worthy developments into the space of Universal Basic Income (UBI) if DeFi models and projects can generate sustainable and sufficient yields for the populace.

Certainly, the future is exciting and the possibilities are endless in this exciting new space of Decentralized Finance!

Remaining Decentralized

Given what you see in the traditional financial system, it's not hard to envision pressure being put on various networks or exchanges to become more centralized. That makes them easier to regulate, provides users with a place to go should something go wrong, etc.

It's also not very hard to imagine that some people will want to skip the slow pathways of existing DeFi networks and be willing to pay for higher-speed access. That provides a way to make money for those who provide access.

It also will end up concentrating wealth and power for those who can afford it. We've already seen it happen with high-frequency trading (HFT) on the NYSE, where traders try to use platforms that are geographically closer to New York to shave off a few nanoseconds. HF traders also invest in hollow-core fiber technology, which moves traffic faster than the fiber optic cables currently used (Osipovich, 2020). They can afford it, and their transactions (which take place via algorithmic trading) can swoop in and eliminate opportunities for other investors.

Move Away From Early Perceptions of Crypto

The only players in the wild wild west of crypto right now are the ones who can afford or think they can afford, to take on the risk. It's more like Las Vegas than it is like New York or London, traditional centers of finance.

Crypto (and to some extent DeFi) is more of a gamble than an investment at the moment. But in Las Vegas, the house always wins. The whole point of decentralization is to remove "the house" from the playing field.

At least DeFi is growing well away from Silk Road and dark web infamy. It needs to continue in that direction to get more average people involved.

Keeping DeFi synonymous with crypto, especially Bitcoin, seems like the wrong move. The very word "crypto" tends to turn average people off. It probably needs to move beyond Bitcoin as well.

Bitcoin and all other PoW networks are not sustainable in our changing climate. The people who don't understand or accept the truth of global, human-driven climate change tend to be Americans. So, while Bitcoin may thrive for a while in the US, other countries (and some Americans) will be looking for solutions that don't require as much fossil fuel or other energy usages.

Bitcoin's mining limit may make sense for people who are afraid of inflation, given that's the underlying reason for the total limit of coins. For people living in a world that hasn't seen much inflation for decades, or only in certain sectors or countries, there's no incentive to use it.

Potentially, inflation could make a big comeback. It is a problem in a few countries, mainly those that don't have strong financial structures already in place. For the nations with central banks and baked-in inflation-fighting mechanisms, protecting against inflation is not the key factor driving financial policy.

Some networks have started using the word token instead of coin, which is helpful because it further distances decentralized finance from its wild west, dark web origins.

Banking and Finance

The financial sector may see the most gain from the implementation of Blockchain technology. Banks are only open on weekdays 5 out of the week. Thus, if you want to deposit a check after 6 p.m. on Friday, you would have to wait until Monday to see the money deposited.

And if you make the deposit within regular business hours, it can take 1 to 3 days to validate the transaction. In contrast, Blockchain never rests. Consumers will have their purchases completed in as few as 10 minutes by incorporating Blockchain into banks, which is the period it takes to connect a block to the Blockchain, independent of holidays or the time of day or week. Banks can now swap funds between entities more easily and safely thanks to Blockchain.

The settling and clearance procedure in the stock market industry, for example, will take up to 3 days (or longer if trading internationally), which means that the money and securities remain frozen at that time. Because of the large amounts involved, even a few days in transit will result in substantial costs and threats for banks. The future savings, according to European bank Santander as well as its research collaborators, range from $15 to $20 billion a year. According to Capgemini, a French consulting firm, Blockchain-based solutions could save customers up to $16 billion in financial and finance fees each year.

Currency

Blockchain is the foundation for cryptocurrencies such as Bitcoin. The Federal Reserve is in control of the US currency. A user's data and currency are legally at the discretion of their bank or government in this central authority scheme. If a user's bank is compromised, their personal details are exposed. The stability of a client's currency may be jeopardized if their bank fails or if they reside in a nation with an authoritarian government. Many of the institutions that went bankrupt in 2008 were partly bailed out by government funds.

These are the concerns that led to the creation and development of Bitcoin. Blockchain enables Bitcoin and other cryptocurrencies to run without the need for a central authority by distributing their activities through a network of computers. This not only lowers risk but also removes a lot of the transaction and delivery costs. It will also have a more secure currency with more applications and a larger network of individuals and institutions for which to do business, both domestically and abroad, for those in states with volatile currencies or financial infrastructures.

For those that may not have state identification, using a cryptocurrency wallet for investment accounts or as a payment method is particularly important. Any country may be in the midst of a civil war, or their governments may lack the necessary resources to provide recognition. Citizens of those countries may be unable to open bank or brokerage accounts, leaving them with little means of securely storing money.

CHAPERT 3:

Blockchain

Blockchain, above all, is a decentralized electronic Blockchain developed on a P2P mechanism that everyone may participate in document transactions that cannot be altered. Adding an additional transaction causes the data to become another block in the chain. A consensus is needed to make changes to the Blockchain because if new data is entered, it cannot be removed.

It is a provable and fully transparent record of every transaction due to it being a write-once, append many technologies. While it offers tremendous benefits, Blockchain adoption is still in its early stages; C-level executives and their business peers can anticipate setbacks in their implementation of the technology, especially with regards to possible vulnerabilities in the applications used on top of the Blockchain.

And it has already been found that it is not the ultimate answer to many tech issues. New consensus protocols and approaches for spacing out the computing and data storage workload to enhance transactional throughput and scalability continue to be proposed by Blockchain standards organizations, universities, and startups.

The Linux Foundation's Hyperled Project has developed a complete suite of software for constructing and managing Blockchain networks. Although a number of companies and developers are focusing on standardizing Blockchain-based applications, there are several who have adopted their own implementations of distributed ledger technologies.

A Blockchain is made up of 3 technologies:

- Blockchain protocol
- Private-key cryptography
- Peer-to-peer network

Let's split each one down into stages, and once you grasp how each one functions, you'll have a far better understanding of the Blockchain craze.

The system worked based on trust because there were consequences to not holding up your end of the bargain. It was also pretty transparent. Whoever needed to know about the transaction would be told. In a small village, as those of you who live in small towns know, there aren't a whole lot of secrets.

There are 3 major aspects to blockchain technology:

1. **Each chain, as the name suggests, is made up of blocks.** A block contains a number of transactions and is encrypted and time-stamped. Every block in the chain references the previous block.

   A major benefit of developing a chain in this way is that it's immediately clear when a block has been tampered with. In order to commit fraud, someone would have to alter all the blocks in the chain, for every version of the chain. Not only is this an extreme amount of work, but it's also very hard work (which we'll get into below).

   Due to this kind of transparency and difficulty in changing the chain, participants can trust the data even when they don't know the identity of the other participants.

   Each participant in the chain has their own identity that shows all their transactions. That maintains the transparency of the chain and allows trust and verification to take place for secure transactions. The ID isn't based on real-world data, so you still have privacy even though the transactions are transparent to all.

2. **Miners are required for new blocks on the chain.**
They are integral to the process of preventing fraud. In real life, have you ever gone to a store with a large denomination like a $100 bill and tried to purchase a small item? You'll notice the cashier hold the bill up to the light, or maybe even check it on a special machine. They're trying to determine if the bill is real, or whether you're trying to pass off a counterfeit and get real bills in exchange.

For money in the physical world, there are a variety of ways to check for counterfeiting. It's harder online where perfect copies can be made and there's no way to verify whether what you have is the original or not.

If the miner verifies that the request is legit, they add it to their list. Every 10 minutes a miner is chosen to add their list, or block, to the blockchain, which keeps the chain up to date.

In order to prevent miners from committing fraud, they compete by guessing what the right number (hash) is, which requires dedicated software. The more powerful a computer that the miner has, the more tries they can make at a hash that results in "winning" the block.

Unlike current platforms and databases where gaining entry to one user (through hacking, bad actors, or whatever) gives access to all the data, someone mining the blockchain needs to spend a lot of time and energy on it.

3. **Nodes connected to the chain maintain its integrity of it.** The ledger is decentralized, so there's no one company, organization, or nation that controls any specific blockchain. Any electronic device can function as a node and keep the network operating. Typically a node is a computer, laptop, or even a server.

The nodes each have their own copy of the blockchain and must approve (via algorithm) any mining to update the blockchain. A full node contains a copy of the entire blockchain.

Once a miner has verified a block, it sends the information to all the nodes on the chain. They check that the block is legitimate, and if so, add it on top of the other blocks on its copy of the chain.

Developers are able to create computer programs that talk to each other on the blockchain. Automating processes allows blockchain technology to expand into a variety of industries, and removes humans and their habits of making mistakes from the operations.

The programming instructions can tell the chain how to perform whatever functionality is required. Everything from musical intellectual property to healthcare records to finance can be executed securely (Builtin, n.d.). Currently, many different industries are learning how to work with and take advantage of blockchain technology.

These programs are known in the DeFi world as smart contracts, and they execute automatically when specific conditions are met on the blockchain. Programs may also be known as DApps (decentralized apps) because they're built on top of decentralized tech. By contrast, apps that you're familiar with from Google Play or Apple Store are mostly centralized, owned by a developer or company.

The whole procedure begins with 2 parties wishing to conduct a trade or 1 party wishing to make a payment to another body. To do that, they'll need:

- Private, secure key
- Public security key

To construct a so-called unique identifier, both of these keys are necessary. Keep in mind that the signature is a complicated combination of numbers, not a handwritten, unique signature. The signature establishes control of the contract and serves as a kind of letter seal. It further proves that the sale is from a reputable source, preventing account holders from making duplicate purchases.

The key sequence solves an authentication problem but does not provide complete protection. It can be used in conjunction with transaction clearance and permits. We'll need a decentralized system to do this.

You will be acquainted with the P2P network if you recall the earlier years of Napster and illicit music downloading. It's a dedicated network that enables 2 people to share items without the involvement of a third party. And, as we all know, the aim of Blockchain and cryptocurrencies is to eliminate the middleman and their interference into the method.

A common trend can be seen by looking at Blockchain. It's a big group of people whose primary goal is to ensure that they all saw the same event at the same moment by validating transactions. And it's open to everyone. They focus on solving a complex mathematical algorithm to protect the network; whoever cracks it first gets to validate the transaction and is awarded a specific cryptocurrency.

Since the whole network and its participants are scattered around the globe, this phase is also known as a decentralized system. Naturally, the larger the network, the safer the transfers are. The combination of a security key and distributed network authentication allows for a safe and fast flow of transactions that can be authenticated in minutes. That's not all; the funds are yet to appear in your bank account. To do so, the network must first define a protocol.

The Blockchain Protocol

We have a block as a result of both of these moves. An encrypted data, stamp, and related details are all included in this interactive element. The block is then distributed to all nodes in the network. The decentralized network is made up of nodes, which are computers that are linked to the network. Each node is made up of a machine and a transaction-validating client.

Nodes serve as the Blockchain technology's "administrators," and they enter willingly. In the end, both of them can be qualified for a prize: a chance to win a Bitcoin or another cryptocurrency. As a result, one person's concern contributes to meeting a public need. The aim of the Bitcoin protocol is to prevent one coin from being used back in 2 separate transactions.

Through resolving proof-of-work mathematical equations, nodes often build and preserve the background of each coin's transactions. If a transaction has been "announced" on the node, all nodes follow the same formula, allowing new blocks or refusing null ones.

Once all nodes have reached an understanding, a new block with a stamped period is added to the chain. Every Blockchain method for verifying each block can be customized. When you think about it, the form and sum of each block will vary because determining if a transaction is legitimate is a question of the Blockchain protocol.

A block is a digital document or activity in the electronic ledger. Whenever a block is finished, it generates a one-of-a-kind safe code that links it to the next. What's the big deal with Blockchain these days? In a nutshell, Bitcoin is a wildly used cryptocurrency that enables payment transfers over an open network utilizing cryptography without revealing individual cryptocurrency owners' identities. When it was established in 2009, it was the first-ever decentralized one.

Other types of cryptocurrencies or virtual money, such as Ether, have also gained momentum and opened up new markets for cross-border monetary transactions.

Satoshi Nakamoto (likely an alias for one or more developers) first coined the word Bitcoin in 2008, when he published a paper about such a peer-to-peer form of digital money that would enable online payments to be transferred directly from one group to another without passing via a finance company.

Public vs. Private Blockchains

Public Blockchain ledgers may be maintained autonomously to share knowledge between parties as a peer-to-peer network with a decentralized timestamping server. An administrator isn't needed. The Blockchain consumers are, in essence, the administrators.

The second type of Blockchain, known called private or validate transactions Blockchain, enables businesses to build and centrally manage their own relational networks, which can be used with collaborators both within and outside the enterprise.

Furthermore, Blockchain networks may be used to create "smart contracts" or business automation scripts that run when such contractual requirements are met. Walmart and IBM, for example, developed a Blockchain-based distribution network to monitor produce from the farm to the table after a bad batch of broccoli made consumers ill with E. coli.

By September 2019, Walmart has requested its produce vendors to enter their data into the Blockchain database. Produce will be efficiently monitored from point to point on the Blockchain using smart contracts, eliminating the need for human interference and mistake.

How Blockchain Redesigns Finance

The currency financial system uses certain justifications to perpetuate itself. You've already read about how everything centers on identity in the modern financial world. The blockchain revises that and places the transaction at the center of everything. That means much of the "value" that the financial system claims to provide is unnecessary.

Here are the key points that modern finance pushes as value drivers and how the blockchain negates all of them.

Attestation

That is the primary pillar on which modern finance is built. "Who" is involved in a transaction is far more important than "what" is being transacted. The financial system claims that verifying identities prevents financial crimes and reduces negative impacts on society. As long as there wasn't any alternative, this pillar is a genuine value-add.

However, this isn't the case anymore. The reason identity is important is because it's the only way we can build trust in a centralized system. If you know who is on the other side of the transaction, you can derive many other data points that build trust. You know where they live, their transaction history, their financial profile, and other important data.

Blockchain changes all of this. For the first time in history, trust isn't built on identity. It doesn't matter who is on the other side of the transaction; the network validates and secures the product or goods being transacted. The record is indelible, and there's no need for an intermediary to validate identities.

Cost

Many commentators wrongly assume that the argument for decentralization is an 'us' versus 'them' topic between proponents of decentralized apps and banks. Banks stand to gain massively from blockchain adoption. Network maintenance and transaction validation are perennial back-office tasks at big banks. The Spanish banking giant Santander reported that they could save $20 billion in annual costs by adopting blockchain networks (Baxi, 2015).

The blockchain automatically validates and maintains transaction records, which eliminates the need for such back-office tasks. Banks can potentially use that money to offer banking services to those who really need them instead of focusing on the rich all the time. Banks earn hefty fees from transaction costs too.

The removal of a bank from a money transfer chain will bring greater value to consumers. The fees that the Bitcoin network charges for a transaction are a small fraction of what banks charge. The result is greater value for a consumer. When the cost savings to banks and lower transaction fees are combined, it's easy to see how small businesses and bootstrapping entrepreneurs benefit from this ecosystem.

Speed

While wire transfer times are now notoriously poor, few people realize that the entire chain of financial settlements takes a long time. For instance, stock market trades take 3 days to settle despite electronic trading occurring in nanoseconds or less. A bank loan trade takes a staggering 23 days to clear. I've already mentioned how your Starbuck latte transaction takes 3 to 4 days to settle.

Banks justify these transfer times by using a variety of arguments. Typically, they're some combination of compliance, network issues, and ledger balancing. All of them are hogwash. In a world where communication occurs instantly, nothing justifies spending 3 or more days clearing a digital transaction. The only explanation is inertia, or worse, an old boy's club that doesn't want to change.

Risk Management

Lengthy transaction times jeopardize our financial system in many ways. The current system has no solution to this problem except huge deposits. The financial crisis in 2008 exposed these systemic risks very well. Ultimately a government bailout, funded by taxpayer dollars, was needed to reduce this risk.

Asset Innovation

High finance often involves the creation of derivatives and other instruments that allow institutions to profit off the moves of any conceivable asset. For instance, it isn't unusual to find Wall Street banks creating derivatives that pay traders out depending on the weather on a certain day. These instruments are often pushed as examples of innovation in the financial industry.

While the value addition of such contracts is debatable, there's no doubt that they are in demand. Centralized systems complicate trading such derivatives and create imbalances in the system since a central party typically sets the price. Unlike stock markets where instruments are regularly traded, these derivatives are opaque, and the market is termed Over the Counter or OTC.

The blockchain is at a similar stage right now as the internet was in the early to mid-1990s. The open-source excitement is slowly being taken over by corporate interests. The Amazons and the Googles of blockchain are coming, and it's interesting to see to what extent the aims of the blockchain will be corrupted.

First off, blockchain and decentralized finance are taking on a sizable adversary in the modern financial system. The big banks have dominated the world for so long that it's unthinkable for them to give up control. One of the ways in which the banks have reasserted control is to simply buy the technology.

For instance, the challenge from fintech upstarts has been met with a wave of capital funding that integrates fintech processes with traditional bank products. That has led to a wave of digital transformation in banks and financial services. The rise of the digital bank has only empowered traditional banks since these are merely online versions of the same services physical banks provide.

Similarly, banks have begun experimenting with the blockchain for their internal processes. In typical big bank fashion, they've begun extracting value but providing none. Given the complexity of the trade settlement process, it was natural that the blockchain would be implemented in this area first by big banks. In 2015, Goldman Sachs filed a patent for a decentralized network powered by a token called SETLCoin that could be used to guarantee same-day trade settlement.

While the technology is impressive and, it certainly makes sense for Goldman's internal workflows, the irony of a Wall Street firm patenting an essentially open-source process, is not lost on blockchain enthusiasts. The corporatization of the blockchain has begun, and it poses interesting questions for decentralization.

Take Blythe Masters, for instance. Masters is a towering figure on Wall Street, one of the few women to break its glass ceilings. Masters built her reputation by building JP Morgan's credit derivatives business from the ground up. In 2012, Masters quit her position at the bank and became the CEO of a small company named Digital Asset Holdings, which aims to provide decentralized network applications to financial institutions.

This network that Masters envisions is endemic to Wall Street veterans who cannot see anything beyond their visions of siloed data. Accessibility is meant to be gated, not democratized. Convenience is meant for those with money, not for the underserved. Take Circle Internet Finance (Circle), for instance.

This company promises to reinvent the way money is stored and sent around the world. Its network is built on the blockchain, which allows for instant settlement and low fees. There are no middlemen. A business can sign up for its service and instantly pay and receive money from around the world, in any currency, without the need for a bank account. Withdrawing money from the network to a physical bank account is currently necessary; however, Circle plans on disrupting the bank by helping entrepreneurs use the blockchain as a store of value, as I previously described. Sounds good so far, doesn't it?

Circle was founded by Jeremy Allaire and Sean Neville, veterans of Silicon Valley. If Wall Street is obsessed with the privacy of its transactions and gating access, Silicon Valley is obsessed with commoditizing data and leveraging it to earn money. Allaire's description of Circle's business adheres to this stereotype.

Circle's services are free for businesses to use. However, as with any technological company, freedom comes at a price. The data that Circle collects will be leveraged to pitch even more products to the user, and that's where Circle will make money. In the future, thanks to the rise of open banking protocols, Circle will undoubtedly share data across third-party members on its network to make money. For instance, Circle could partner with a bank and sell them your data. The bank can then tailor credit cards and loan offerings to you while on Circle's network.

The aims of the blockchain are completely corrupted by companies such as these. There's no question of Circle's network being made open. It is a permission-based network, and somehow, its founders have managed to turn their blockchain-based product into a data mine. The very thing that the blockchain is meant to overcome is Circle's primary aim.

People like Masters, Allaire, and Neville are quintessential examples of executives championing a centralized system. Having profited from them, there's no way they can envision giving it up, even if it means corrupting the technology that is meant to replace dinosaurs like them.

That doesn't mean that blockchain is doomed. There are no small number of decentralized apps in development that don't rely on such puny visions. The Ethereum blockchain is the most active when it comes to app development. Currently, the blockchain is being used to store land registry records and other financial data. Users can participate in cryptocurrency networks that pay dividends, much like a savings account will pay the interest every year. Regulation is always an issue with decentralized networks. While the individuals previously mentioned show how decentralization can be absorbed by a centralized network, to its detriment, complete decentralization is also a bad thing. Bitcoin's early days proved how decentralized networks could be corrupted by nefarious actors. Some degree of regulation is a good thing.

Finding the balance between decentralization and regulation is a major challenge. There's no doubt that the likes of Wall Street and Silicon Valley will corrupt the idea of decentralization and create private networks that reduce access. However, the majority of the blockchain is open source and, this holds a lot of promise for the average person. It remains to be seen how financial services evolve. Currently, visions like the one Masters has is the same pattern of patching new tech onto old systems. How will real innovation emerge in this sector? No one has the roadmap as of yet, but the future is exciting nonetheless.

CHAPERT 4:

Crypto

T rading is very risky, irrespective of what you are trading. If you want to make money from crypto all you have to do is to register for a blockchain course, get a certificate, get a job in the crypto space and chances are they will pay you a lot of money because this is a new field. Blockchain is a digital record of transactions where transactions are recorded with a stable cryptographic signature and the records are duplicated and distributed across the entire network of computer systems for security purposes. This simply means that when you buy a house with cryptocurrency such as Bitcoin, you don't have to go to the bank anymore to do a transaction, you can just buy a house on your phone and your transaction will be recorded and stored on the blockchain which is a digital ledger/record.

Basics of Cryptocurrency

Before there were smart contracts, blockchain tech was used to send and receive crypto. This is digital money that can be used to buy and sell online, or traded for profit. Many companies issue their own crypto in the form of tokens that you can swap for their products and services.

There are a ton of different cryptocurrencies currently available. As of February 2021, there were about 7,300 different "coins" and a total value of about $1.6 trillion (Royal et al, 2021). You might be familiar with the OG token, Bitcoin. New crypto appears regularly through initial coin offerings (ICOs).

Unlike currencies such as the dollar, euro, and British pound, there are no central banks that affect the performance of crypto. A country or entity's central bank may have a mandate (such as fighting inflation) that affects the value of the currency but has nothing to do with free-market forces. Some users like crypto for this reason.

Like all currencies, crypto doesn't generate any cash flow. At the moment, investing in crypto is mainly for speculators who want to sell at a profit. For currencies to be widely accepted, they must have some stability so people can figure out what a fair price is for any given product or service. It's hard to do that when the value of the currency fluctuates wildly, which has been true of crypto since the beginning.

People who want to get involved in crypto need an online wallet to hold their investments. An unfortunate number of investors have lost significant amounts of cryptocurrency because they forgot the password to their digital wallets! That number could be as high as 20% of the total value for Bitcoin (Campbell, 2021). The digital wallet is similar to a bank account online, except much harder to hack—or get into if you forget your password.

Cryptocurrencies, DApps, and blockchain are all part of DeFi, or the push to make every financial service that you can think of global, decentralized, and transparent. You can think of it as financial applications created on top of the blockchain.

Savings, borrowing money, insurance, and trading can all be done without the intermediaries and institutions that are integral to today's world of money. Instead of running financial checking and savings accounts through the banks, anyone in the world can access money as long as they have a phone and Internet connection.

In the next chapter, we'll delve into the DeFi advantages more specifically. They result from the differences between decentralized finance (sometimes called open finance) and the centralized systems that are currently in use.

There's no central bank dictating limits on a cryptocurrency, or banking institution making the rules about who has access to their funds. Instead, smart contracts or computer code maintain the rules. In addition to cutting out the intermediary cost, allowing smart contracts means that the tech can basically run itself without a lot of human interference.

In practical terms, developers need to maintain their DApps with bug fixes or upgrades, just like other software programmers. There's no reason, though, that a transaction must go through multiple levels of human approval.

- **Global functionality.** Most (current) applications and financial systems software are designed for the major currencies in play and their organizations, namely the Euro, US dollar, British pound, and Chinese renminbi/yuan.

  DApps, by contrast, are designed to work globally. Cryptocurrencies are in global use around the world. Bitcoin is Bitcoin whether you're located in the US, Zimbabwe, or Uruguay.

- **No gatekeepers.** DApps are "permissionless" by design so that anyone can use and create them. No forms to fill out, online or off. All you need is your online wallet. There are no "accredited investors" when it comes to crypto or any other DeFi possibility.

- **Can build on each other.** Because the programs are all open-source, developers can mix and match what's already out there to create a new product. There's no intellectual property protection to navigate if you want to use something that DeFi has already created.

- **Independent.** In the traditional world, there's what's known as "open banking." Third-party financial software providers can get access to data held at financial institutions such as banks through APIs or application programming interfaces. This allows companies to integrate data held in different places to provide new solutions for their customers.

In the beginning, cryptocurrencies had no collateral behind them. In this, they're very similar to the US dollar once it was removed from the gold standard, and the euro and British pound, which all "float." As crypto has matured, however, stablecoins have developed which are pegged to some reference, often collateral such as the US dollar.

In theory, stablecoins shouldn't fluctuate as wildly as other crypto does. In practice, there's more volatility than most investors want, though that may be due to how young the technology is.

Lending platforms have also started to grow through DeFi, and they provide a measure of privacy that traditional lending doesn't. If you want to borrow money from a traditional lender, they'll scrape up your credit score and history, maybe look at your tax returns depending on the type of loan, and ask for an income history.

If you borrow using DeFi, on the other hand, all you need is collateral, typically some form of crypto. It doesn't matter what your credit score is or how much you make in income or who you are as long as you have the collateral. Most DeFi runs on the Ethereum platform which allows for smart contracts (Bitcoin does not), so usually the collateral is in the form of ether, which is the platform's cryptocurrency.

How Cryptocurrency Markets Work

Many see crypto trading as the Wild West of markets because of its lack of regulations. While it means that you will not be slowed down by many rules and strict enforcement that are followed on Wall Street, it also means that there is more of a risk. You are not looked after as much as you are when trading traditional stocks, at least not by a major and heavily-financed governmental agency. The crypto market can change suddenly because of supply and demand and there will not be as many precautions put into place to rescue you if things go south. You need to be extra careful—and extra confident—when trading in crypto. Simply put, if things go in the wrong direction and you make a great fall, there is no net below to catch you. The lack of regulations can be both a good and a bad thing.

As stated, supply and demand are the biggest engines driving the major changes in the cryptocurrency market. The number of coins in circulation and the desire of others to get their hands on them is really what spikes the price of the coins. That is an easy concept to wrap your head around and keep in mind as you start your trading career. What other factors play into the value of crypto? There are a few.

Outside Events

The crypto market isn't immune to scandal and security breaches and general economic uncertainty. Any of those things can cause people to buy or sell their coins and can affect the market in some major ways. If the global economy hits a rough patch, you may see the value of crypto plummet as people sell what they have to secure currency that feels more "real" or easier to hold onto in a traditional bank. If there is a major scandal related to crypto or a security breach that shows its weaknesses, you may see people fleeing from crypto for a while for the same reasons. When people get scared, they sell. When they sell, the value goes down.

Market Integration

This is a major factor when you are talking about the value of cryptocurrencies. As cryptocurrencies grow in popularity, many mainstream businesses and markets want to be involved with them. Over the last few years, there have been instances of crypto integration in some major ways. Certain businesses have started to accept crypto as a form of payment, many websites have started too as well. When this happens more and more, it will only make more people interested in getting a piece of crypto and that will drive up the value of your investment. Make sure to keep an eye on the latest developments in the world of cryptocurrency and try to have an understanding of the business side of things and how well crypto is expanding in the world.

The Press

The media has always been wary of Bitcoin and other cryptocurrencies. Ever since the inception of Bitcoin, many in the press have not known how to handle or report on crypto. To this day, their stories are sometimes slanted or confused and can paint cryptocurrencies in a negative light. These news stories could damage the reputation of crypto and could lead to a lack of demand or a sell-off of certain coins. Crypto is not immune to nasty headlines.

Crypto Tokens

In the digital currency environment, the terms cryptocurrencies, crypto tokens, and altcoins are often used interchangeably. Cryptocurrency, on the other hand, is the superset, with altcoins and crypto tokens as subsets. The most common cryptocurrency is Bitcoin, which is a form of currency used for making or accepting transfers on the Blockchain. Alternative cryptocurrencies, or altcoins, were created in the aftermath of Bitcoin's huge popularity.

Alternative coins of Bitcoins are referred to as "altcoins." They were introduced as improved Bitcoin replacements, claiming to eliminate some of Bitcoin's drawbacks. Altcoins include Litecoin, Digital Currencies, Namecoin, and Dogecoin, to name a few.

Despite differing degrees of success, none have achieved the amount of prominence that Bitcoin does. Crypto tokens are fungible and tradable assets or utilities that are sometimes generated by an initial coin offering on a Blockchain.

- Cryptocurrencies are virtual coins that are used to promote cryptocurrency transfers (making and accepting payments).
- Crypto tokens and Altcoins are two distinct kinds of cryptocurrencies.
- Crypto tokens are a form of cryptocurrency that reflects a particular commodity or usage and are stored on a blockchain.
- Crypto tokens, which are created by an initial coin offering, are often used to collect funds for crowd purchases.

Crypto tokens, also known as crypto properties, are customized digital currency tokens that reflect an asset or utility and are stored on their own blockchains. They are more often used to collect funds for crowd transactions, but they may also be seen in other ways. For example, on a blockchain which used to handle certain data for a retail chain, one may provide crypto tokens that reflect X amount of consumer loyalty points.

Another crypto token may be issued that entitles the holder to see 10 hours of live material on a multimedia blockchain. Another crypto token may also reflect other cryptocurrencies, like 15 bitcoins on a specific blockchain. These crypto tokens are exchangeable and transferable across the blockchain's numerous participants. In essence, altcoins and cryptocurrencies are digital tokens with their own specific Blockchains that are mostly used as a means of making digital payments.

Crypto tokens, on the other side, are built on top of a blockchain, which serves as a platform for the development and implementation of decentralized applications and smart contracts, with the tokens serving as a means of payment. The basic initial coin offering procedure, which includes a crowdfunding exercise to finance project creation, is used to produce, distribute, sell, and circulate crypto tokens.

These crypto-assets are often used as transaction units on blockchains that are built utilizing standard models, such as the Ethereum network's token creation tool. Smart contracts or autonomous frameworks are used to handle and control the different transactions that exist on the network of such Blockchains.

What Is Bancor?

Bancor is a decentralized protocol that enables consumers to transfer virtual currency tokens quickly and accurately rather than trading them on cryptocurrency exchanges such as Coinbase. Bancor Network Token is the only cryptocurrency in the Bancor network.

BNT is the 109th most expensive cryptocurrency by market cap as of February 2021, with a total valuation of about $212 million and a price of $1.88 per BNT.

Bancor is a decentralized finance network that aims to offer liquidity and returns to small-and micro-cap coins.

Bancor and its rival Uniswap are the pioneers of a modern generation of decentralized financial networks, using two token layers to promote its liquidity reserves and usability: ETHBNT and BNT.

In a recent generation of open finance networks, Bancor and its rival Uniswap are the frontrunners.

Bancor is an Ethereum-based on-chain trading protocol that allows automatic, decentralized trading through several Blockchains. Galia Benartzi, Eyal Hertzog and Guy Benartzi first created the protocol in Israel in 2017.

Bancor, according to their whitepaper, allows for automated price determination and autonomous liquidity for tokens in smart contract Blockchain technology. Bancor was selected as a nod to John Maynard Keynes, who suggested the term "Bancor" for a supranational reserve currency at the Bretton Woods conference.

Bancor's Crypto Liquidity Pools

Given their market valuation and if they're not classified on an exchange, several tiny cryptocoins are illiquid. Transaction fees might be greater than those of the more liquid currencies, such as Bitcoin and Ethereum. Small-and micro-cap coins may be purchased and exchanged with limited hassle and fees thanks to Bancor's smart token and smart contract technologies.

Smart tokens and smart contracts are self-executing contracts with ideal conditions between parties involved written into lines of code. A typical cryptocurrency trade on a centralized or decentralized cryptocurrency exchange entails the exchanging of tokens between two or more parties: a buyer and a seller, with the exchange serving as a market maker.

Bancor Network Token (BNT)

Bancor's goal is to cut out the middleman by providing a decentralized reserve currency, the Bancor Network Token (BNT), as well as an automated exchange system that regulates rates and trading volumes via the protocol. The default currency for all smart tokens generated on the Bancor network is BNT, Bancor's native reserve currency token.

One of the commitments made during BNT's initial coin offering (ICO) was that investors would earn interest on conversion costs as other crypto coins were exchanged into and out of BNT. Bancor's protocol allows users to switch between ERC-20 compliant tokens. Smart contracts that carry reserves of many other ERC-20 tokens are connected to each smart token. Internally, the tokens are allocated dependent on these stocks and the number of consumer queries.

Smart tokens are essentially virtual coins that store the financial value of other associated virtual coins. It works in the same way as a central bank that keeps foreign exchange reserves and exchanges them as required. Both virtual currency tokens that are compliant with the ERC-20 format are supported by the Bancor protocol. Any smart token developed on the Bancor network is ERC-20 compliant, which means it can interact with another token on the network.

CHAPERT 5:

How You Can Start Using DeFi Right Now and Why You Should

Opportunities to Make Money from DeFi Right Now

W e're not quite to the decentralized utopia yet, as you know. The technology isn't as widespread as it needs to be for that to happen, and there are some problems that need solutions before the general public is ready. Yet there are still opportunities for you to profit from what currently exists.

Obviously, if you have the answer to one of these problems, you can probably get some funding to turn that into reality.

As a non-technical person or someone who has other things to do besides watch crypto feed all day, you can still make money from it. Some require more effort on your part, but others just take a little set-up time at first.

Active

1. **Arbitrage.** One benefit to illiquid and relatively thin markets is that you have more opportunity for arbitrage than in a big market where the law of large numbers mostly eliminates it. In general, arbitrage refers to buying and selling the same asset in different marketplaces to make money from price differentials.

   One way to make money is known as yield arbitrage, where you look at different loans or staked assets. The rates fluctuate widely and there's not a lot of competition to narrow the spreads (differences) between them.

   The other method of profit is across the exchanges, to take advantage of price differentials for the currencies.

   You'll need to do your due diligence on the asset you're working with and keep an eye on prices, so this strategy does require you to hang out in front of your computer watching the trades. They're short-lived, so if you don't make the trade when you see it, you might miss it.

   Also, be aware that there are crypto bots that act in the same way as HFTs on the stock exchange, which may make arbitrage on a dex harder.

2. **Options.** If you think a particular token is likely to increase in value, or decrease, or a relatively short period of time, you can buy an option on it to profit from your belief.

   While arbitrage doesn't require you to have an opinion on the asset (all you're doing is looking for mismatched prices or interest rates), option buying does. It's theoretically possible to construct an advanced strategy using puts and calls that will profit as long as the asset is moving, but that may be too expensive to pull off in an illiquid market.

Passive

1. **Staking.** You learned about staking in an earlier chapter. By locking (or staking) your tokens into a smart contract, you earn additional tokens as a reward. Just as with traditional finance systems, you may need to either stake for an extended period of time, or deposit a minimum amount in order to earn rewards.

2. **Provide liquidity.** In DeFi, LPs are liquidity providers. (An LP is something entirely different when it comes to traditional finance or law!) You contribute your tokens to a pool that enables swaps between your token and

another and earn interest (in the form of the token) for supplying your liquidity.

You're not guaranteed a profit this way, because if one of the tokens loses a significant amount of value, you'll lose value, too. You can get data from aggregators to help you decide which pools are more likely to be profitable.

Getting into a (relatively) more liquid pool with less volatile assets will also help you hedge the risk of loss.

3. **Yield farming.** Once you've become an LP, you can lock the tokens you received (as a reward for being an LP) into a yield farm. Basically, you're earning interest on your interest.
   You need to be careful about the yield farm you use, however, because some of them can be unscrupulous about stealing LP tokens. Use a platform that's been established for some time and has been externally audited.

4. **Lending.** As you know, in exchange for lending your tokens you can earn interest on them. Because loans are usually overcollateralized, you don't need to be as concerned about whether you'll get your money back, compared to P2P loans in the traditional system.

5. **Buy and hold (or hodl).** Technically, this isn't a passive income stream as the options above are. If you choose to

buy an asset whose price rises over time, you can sell it for a profit in the future. In the DeFi arena, this is more speculative, as opposed to an investment in a company, for example.

Will the Nyan Cat NFT ultimately be more valuable than the NFT of the first Tweet? Who knows? But you may find a digital artist you like, and buy their NFTs, as art collectors do with paintings and sculptures. Or you may bet on a token to be left standing after the industry consolidates at some future point in time.

CHAPERT 6:

How to Invest in DeFi

I n order to get into DeFi investments, first, we need to know some tools where to buy cryptocurrencies. These are the 3 main ones, let's know their advantages and disadvantages.

Binance

This is a platform for exchanging cryptocurrencies, is one of the most used in the world. It was launched in July 2017. It has an ICO to finance the development of the Exchange. This allows the platform not to depend on venture capital companies, being funded by the community.

Binance launched its ICO on July 3 and put up for sale 100 million ERC20 tokens called BNB (Binance Coin). It lasted just 3 minutes and managed to raise $15 million. 11 days after launching the ICO the Exchange was already available.

There were many registered users after the launch, which generated some access problems due to the large volume of users. Today it is valued at more than 2 billion dollars.

Bit2Me

Founded in 2014, it specializes in financial technology. It has a great knowledge in blockchain technology and cryptocurrencies, helping individuals, exchanges, mining pools, issuing tokens, investment funds, governments, and institutions, trading and managing different digital assets in an optimal way.

It serves as a gateway to frictionless markets, rendering the traditional financial system obsolete. It was created with the vision of transparency and open and efficient financial systems. It supports many initiatives in the DeFi system, interacting with protocols, providing liquidity, and participating in networks that encompass decentralized lending, trading, and other financial applications.

The entire system is developed internally by its operators and considers both a technological and commercial enterprise, creating products, processes, and tools to change the world, with the goal of enabling frictionless, fair, and transparent markets.

You have to create an account, before trading, you have to go through a data validation process. It is a process that you achieve quickly. To be able to use it you need to have set up the profile well, filled in all the data, and attached your ID. It is an important step in this kind of platform.

Coinbase

It is a great platform that offers you many advantages. Among them, you can see the graphs with the evolution of prices, you can know how the value of the cryptocurrencies you have goes up or down. Let's analyze this platform in detail.

It acts as a digital wallet, which means that you can use it to store your cryptocurrencies in a unified place. Think of it like your bank's app, where you can see the number of cryptocurrencies you have and the value of their evolution. Also, each wallet will also have a unique address with which others can send cryptocurrencies to it, allowing you to receive or make payments with them without having to go through other services.

With this, you have a service whose operation is very similar to others such as PayPal (something that Binance and Bit2Me do not yet allow) or your bank's app. You can manage them as if it were a stock market app, but instead of speculating on the market, you can do it with the cryptocurrency market.

The company is based in San Francisco, California, was founded in 2012 by Brian Armstrong and Fred Ehrsam. BBVA has been one of the major investors. It has more than 30 million users.

Coinbase charges you commissions when you buy or sell cryptocurrencies, when buying you have a commission of 1.49%, and when selling to convert them into fiat money, the commission is 1%. What it does not have is commission on transfers of assets to other virtual wallets.

To register is very easy, you just need to be of legal age, give the service the name, surname, email, and password, you can make use of the account. Then you link another payment method that can be a PayPal account, bank, credit, or debit card.

Coinbase can be used on mobile or on the website. You can see the fiat money value of your investments, the evolution of the main cryptos, and decide which ones you want to be shown to you, seeing a summary of the outstanding news of the sector. There is a button called Trade, where you can buy, sell or convert cryptocurrencies. In any of the cases before accepting the operation will always appear the commission you have to pay so that everything is clear to you.

How to Invest: Using DeFi Technologies for Investment Opportunities

Given the industry's nascency, many of these strategies contain significant risk (detailed in the section titled "Risk Factors" below) and require sophisticated technical knowledge to execute.

1. Borrowing and Lending

Suppose you own a small business and need a loan for whatever reason. Unfortunately, they don't let you just walk into the Small Business Administration and walk out with bags full of unmarked bills for you to disburse as you see fit. The SBA facilitates getting a loan, but it's still underwritten by a financial institution most of the time. You're just adding on another layer with the SBA because they vet your business before finding an appropriate lender.

DeFi Lending

DeFi lending, which involves a user depositing funds into a protocol, is similar to a typical fund deposit or investment that pays interest over time. Lenders get not just interest on their digital funds but also a governance token or DAI as a bonus: Compound COMP, Aave produces LEND, and Maker offers DAI. The 3 to 5% interest rate for lending is better than many banks for ordinary customers, but it may not be sufficient to offset the ever-present danger of smart contract abuses. On the other hand, these rates look to be highly appealing to high-capital investors, hedge funds, or institutions, especially when applied to stablecoins like USDT, USDC, or DAI. Lending may also assist in minimizing the risks of market fluctuations by allowing users to make money without having to trade.

DeFi Borrowing

The majority of funds on a lending platform aren't there just to earn interest. Becoming a lender is just a small part of the equation; the true magic occurs when considering the range of options available to lenders. However, first and foremost, it's critical to comprehend collateral.

The usage of decentralized technologies does not need authorization. As a result, traditional assessments such as credit score, equity, or income cannot be used to establish a safe loan amount. Lending sites, on the other hand, demand borrowers to provide cryptocurrency assets as collateral. Over-collateralization is a common feature of DeFi loans. This implies that participants can only collect a part of the collateral they have provided: When you lend $10,000 in ETH, you could get up to $7,500 in DAI or other assets (roughly 75% of your collateral). This may sound paradoxical at first, but it's important to verify that all users can repay their loan; the collateralized assets may be liquidated when you can't repay the loan.

2. Insurance

Insurers won't need ID proofs or any other sensitive data to verify who you are. Relevant information is already present on the network, and all they need to do is access publicly available transaction data. The insurance contract can be sent as another smart contract that involves all parties and is secured by a multi-sig.

Thus, the whole experience is peer-driven, and dAirbnb facilitates this connection. It doesn't sit in the middle collecting rent for the privilege of offering you a connection to some other party.

DeFi platforms have manifested out of a desire to disrupt intermediaries in financial services. In doing so, the elimination/reduction in counterparty risk has led to a substantial increase in "software risk." Given the nascence of the market and lack of audit history, there are numerous blind spots in the industry's future growth. Decentralized insurance has emerged as a potential solution; however, the depth of liquidity and clarity on payout logistics remains uncertain.

3. Open Network Companies

Decentralizing the structure of an organization has other effects too. For starters, the amount of capital needed to compete in the marketplace is reduced considerably. If someone wants to create a platform that has better features than dAirbnb, all they need to do is establish connections to apps in the ecosystem and develop their app to the best of their abilities.

Given the open-source nature of the blockchain, it opens everyone up for competition, and big companies cannot buy their way forward. For example, Google currently buys any company that can even remotely develop a better search algorithm than them. That is to stave off competition. Most owners sell to Google because the prospect of going up against a trillion-dollar behemoth that effectively controls the internet is a losing prospect.

Similar patterns play themselves out in social media networking and technology. For instance, Apple has walled its app store off completely from other networks in the name of security and holds developers captive to its demands. The internet was meant to be an open marketplace, free for everyone to compete, but big corporations have captured their corners of it and will never let go.

The blockchain brings greater efficiency to the market thanks to decentralization. Companies can reduce their internal search costs as previously described, and this leads to the creation of novel business models. Here are some possible ventures that we might see in the future.

4. Autonomous Agents

When talking of companies, we think of corporations that have employees, offices, servers, and so on. What if the company can be fully automated via a smart agent that roams a decentralized network, making deals that benefit the organization, updating itself to account for competition, and incorporating new products to serve customers better?

Smart contracts are more than just lines of code. They can be taught to do literally anything. Currently, technology limits us from automating them beyond a few simple tasks. A lot of automation comes in the form of validation against existing conditions. However, nothing is stopping smart contracts from learning and interacting with a larger ecosystem.

5. Art Creation

While the internet did a great deal to bring information to the masses, it never managed to compensate the people who created that information. The downfall of newspapers and publishing houses and the takeover of nonsensical Buzzfeed-like websites is one of the many ways the internet affected media consumption.

Currently, content creators have to use centralized platforms to spread their message. For example, an aspiring journalist has to maintain a blog, a Twitter account, and a Facebook profile to source and report stories. In addition, their stories appear on a website that exercises further control over output. In most cases, content creators lose rights to their work and don't get compensated for how often it gets shared or consumed.

The blockchain enables creators to digitally sign their art and lease their artwork to other consumers. Non-fungible tokens or NFTs have become hot recently, and speculators have rushed in increasing the prices of everything. While the speculative boom shows how little people understand blockchain technology, the NFT itself is a smart contract that can change the way creators collect royalties.

Aside from helping artists, the blockchain will also eliminate fraud. Currently, the art world is inundated with fakes that cost a ton of resources to verify and discredit. Insurance companies build entire business lines insuring art and verifying authenticity. The blockchain will simplify all of this since the record of a piece of art will be immutably stored on the network.

Verifying its origin and creation will be simple. Even if a single record is lost, its existence is stored on the entire network and can thus be restored easily.

6. Cooperative Companies

The word sharing implies a free exchange of goods and services. Think of kids sharing toys. Uber and Airbnb don't offer people the chance to share anything. An Uber driver is a taxi operator at the end of the day and has to pay Uber a cut of their earnings for the privilege.

The blockchain can reinvent the so-called sharing economy of today by turning it into an actual peer-driven network. You've already read about how such decentralized platforms would work, so I won't dive into the details again. There's no doubt that such DApps give users greater control over their data and business models. As such, if the price of this control is the obsolescence of centralized platforms, then it's worth it.

A side-effect of the blockchain is that it can turn a sharing economy into a metered economy. For instance, when you hire a car these days, it's tough to hire one for a few hours. You'll probably be charged for an entire day no matter how little you need the car. The reason is it's tough to locate renters for the remaining hours of the day and enforce rental terms over short periods.

Zipcar made waves when it allowed people to rent cars hourly. However, this platform didn't really add any value. It merely aggregated people who were willing to rent their cars when the vehicles were lying unused. The blockchain doesn't have a billion-dollar valuation but delivers far more value than Zipcar claims to do.

By tying rental terms to smart contracts and linking with a decentralized review app, a company could create a system where people can rent their cars when unused easily. Identities will be verified by the network and contract terms will be enforced automatically. Owners will need to physically check their vehicles for damage, of course; that cannot be automated away.

The possibilities are endless. We could sublease our WiFi hotspots, storage capacity, even the heat generated by our computers. The only question is how creative can we get when it comes to monetizing our assets?

CHAPERT 7:

Which Problem DeFi Solves?

Transparency

J ust to be clear, transparency doesn't mean that everyone else on the blockchain can see what you personally have done or invested in. Users are identified by a string of alphanumeric characters that can't be traced to you in real life. Even if you and I are on the same blockchain, you can't see that I, Eugene McKinney, have bought so much Ether or used Bitcoin to invest in online real estate. You can see that so much Ether was purchased by a user, but you can't tell who the user is.

It's a bit like watching the stock ticker because share prices are updated to reflect the latest trading activity. There is an important difference, however: on the ticker, you can't see who bought stock in AAAA. You'll just see the price and number of shares traded move. On the blockchain, you can see all the transactions occurring as soon as mined blocks are authenticated and verified.

Why is that such an advantage? For one thing, it cuts down significantly on fraud. This is excellent for financial operations because it makes audits much easier. No such thing as the keeping of two ledgers (one real and one for busybodies), because everyone has all the same access to the information. Every transaction can be traced—no shuffling around between business entities and conveniently "losing" a little here and a little there.

It can also revolutionize gaming and predictive markets where users bet on anything from who will win the next large sports contest to the next large national election to all kinds of other gambles. Having "provable fairness" might induce more players to the games because they wouldn't be concerned about having the deck stacked against them (HBUS, 2018). When it comes to casinos, online or off, the house is always in favor but players can check to make sure that their results are fair and real.

Interoperability

Like a pile of Legos, developers can take DApps that have already been made and add them to new apps or change apps to their liking. In this way, users have a more seamless experience moving money around or performing transactions for a variety of needs. It creates the opportunity to develop completely new applications on the blockchain.

Another facet of interoperability has yet to be realized, which is to be able to move from one blockchain technology to another. For example, suppose you have Bitcoin and want to buy something on the Ethereum network. Currently, developers are working on how to standardize some of the protocols so that it doesn't matter what platform you use, you can move about in the DeFi world.

Another potential solution is to hook them together via APIs, as traditional finance does now. There are some authenticity concerns with this method, however, not to mention that it requires the platforms to connect one-to-one rather than forming a network or consortium.

Independence from Traditional Financial Structures

Many modern money applications are strictly regulated, especially in the US and Europe. At first, plenty of early adopters latched onto crypto as a way to escape financial scrutiny and to make purchases on the "dark web." Sites on the dark (or "deep") web are typically encrypted in a way that they don't appear on traditional search engines.

Many of these sites are perfectly legal, such as private files hosted on secure document sites like Dropbox and its competitors. It's also used by political dissidents from authoritarian countries that restrict such activities to prevent them from being tossed in jail.

There is, however, illegal activity on the dark web, such as the trading of stolen credit card numbers and buying drugs in areas where they're not legalized. You can see why someone who's dealing with illicit affairs would prefer to keep their search activity anonymous and pay for their products and services in a way that's untraceable to all but the most sophisticated cybersecurity teams.

Having said all that, being independent of traditional finance is of huge benefit to many people around the world who don't have access to capital, typically those living in less developed countries or who are below the poverty line in developed ones.

As an example, in order to trade stocks in the US, you typically need a checking account from an accredited financial institution like a bank, credit union, or brokerage firm to begin with. The usual way to open up such an account is to go there in person, show your government-issued ID and proof of residence and fill out a number of documents. Technology has made it possible for people to fill out documents online, but it's also often difficult to do over mobile technology so it's best to have an Internet connection.

Many banks charge fees just to have the account open unless you can set up a direct deposit into the account on a regular basis. In other words, just to open an account, you need an address where you can prove that you're living (with a utility bill in your name or some such), a tablet or laptop, and a stable internet connection or bank branch in your location.

In the US, residents of poorer neighborhoods are typically "unbanked" because there are too many barriers to opening a bank account. Many financial institutions don't have a presence in these neighborhoods at all.

Workers often go to the payday loan place to cash their checks, which takes a huge bite out of their money, to begin with. Payday loan shops serve these customers by being available early in the morning and late at night, and not requiring much in the way of Internet connections or documents to hand over the cash they need to pay bills.

For similar reasons, many people in developing countries don't have access to traditional money structures either. The banks don't exist at all, or they're known to be untrustworthy. Internet connection may be spotty or nonexistent, depending on location.

When just trying to access money from your paycheck is so difficult, imagine how hard everything else is as well. In the US, the wealth of the middle class tends to be concentrated in their homes as assets. Depending on where you live, it might be impossible to save up enough money to buy a house outright, so you need to take out a mortgage.

If you've ever done that, you know how much of a nightmare it is. You need a solid credit score, which means you need to have credit in the first place. You'll show the bank your tax returns, pay stubs to verify your income, and sign off on pages and pages of documents. If you're counting any other income (such as spousal support) you have to document that as well. The house itself must meet certain standards for conventional loans.

Not only are you faced with paying interest for years on end, but you also have to come up with a down payment and more fees for a single transaction than you've ever seen in your life. The bank usually makes you pay for the loan process itself (loan origination fee). You'll also pay for the title search and documentation, your real estate agent (if you have one), the escrow agent who holds your money, etc.

All that documentation can be very hard for the unbanked to come by, even if they've regularly been making rent payments. People without a credit card might find it hard to find an affordable loan because they don't have credit in their name and therefore no credit history. Again, this can be true even if they pay their other bills on time.

Yet there are many reasons why the unbanked should have the same access to capital as middle-class people in developed countries with stable jobs and internet access. There are plenty of budding entrepreneurs in undeveloped countries and unbanked locations who could use a small start-up loan. Anyone can learn how to trade stocks, so why should someone be held back because they don't have a checking account?

Blockchain technology and crypto provide a path to money that people need without demanding the same infrastructure. With a little knowledge, a mobile phone, and an online wallet, which most people across the globe do have access to, anyone can engage in DeFi and get the banking, loans, and other financial products they need. No need to visit anyone or line up reams of documents or prove that they live where they claim to live.

Low Service Costs

In addition to not needing the same expensive infrastructure, DeFi provides more people with access to capital without having to pay all the fees that go along with the entities inside that infrastructure. Even a basic checking account often comes with a fee to open it up, a monthly fee to keep it going, a fee to issue the debit card, a fee for printing checks, and a fee for overdrawing your account (pulling out more money than is actually in the account.) If you're interested in trading securities or purchasing investments, there's a fee for opening up your brokerage account and various other fees. If one of your accounts is a retirement account (such as an IRA here in the US), expect to pay an additional fee for its administration too. Any type of loan comes with fees, plus the interest you're expected to pay on the principal (original amount) of the loan itself. Each time your transaction passes through someone's hands in traditional finance, your cost of transaction increases in terms of both money and time. Middlemen must be paid!

When you want to take out a loan to buy a house, you'll talk to a loan officer, who probably has to pass your documentation on to their manager to sign off on it. Then it goes to the underwriter, who can take weeks or months to determine how much of a credit risk you are and what interest rate you should be charged. They'll likely need to send that to their department manager for approval before they contact you. That's at least 4 different touches on your loan, and all 4 pairs of hands need to be paid.

Removing intermediaries not only simplifies access to capital but makes it cheaper, too. Having DApps that process information instead of people results in getting your money faster. Transparent rules and policies mean that you don't show up at your bank with a fistful of documents, only to find out that you're missing a key piece of information. Instead, you know what's necessary ahead of time. You can also see that it's a fair process because it's so transparent.

Global Solutions

There's no real reason other than current infrastructure that people should only access capital from the country that they live in, or buy things from the country (or region) that they live in. Wealthy people can easily buy whatever they want across the world, and hire someone to do all the tedious work to make that possible. The rest of us don't live in that reality.

Most of us have difficulty buying products and services in other countries (unless we're using a global purchasing site, and even sometimes that throws a wrench in the process). If you live in the US, Eurozone, or UK, the currency exchange usually isn't much of a problem. If you live elsewhere or want to buy something elsewhere, strap in for the ride!

The US and most other developed countries use fiat currency. That means that there's no collateral backing the money; it has no intrinsic value. Up until the 1970s, the US dollar was backed by gold, but America went off the gold standard during that decade. The value of gold fluctuates mightily, so going back to the gold standard won't make the dollar or any other currency more stable.

Fiat money gives the Fed more leniency when it comes to controlling inflation (which was a massive problem in the 20th Century but not so much in the 21st, yet.) The Fed can affect the supply and demand for the dollar, which means it has more weapons against inflation.

The exchange rates between fiat currencies float according to supply and demand. When you can buy more British pounds with a US dollar, Americans can buy more things from the UK and take trips over there. By contrast, when you buy more dollars with a British pound, the UK will import more from the US, so American companies benefit.

Supply and demand ebb and flow due to a variety of factors, but one of them is certainly what the global reserve currency is. The Bretton Woods agreement after WWII established the US dollar as the world's reserve currency (Amadeo, 2020).

Another method of establishing a national currency is to peg it to another country's currency. Nations that use a dollar peg keep their currency at a fixed exchange rate to the US dollar. While most nations that peg to another currency use the dollar, the second most popular type is a euro peg. Usually, a country with a dollar peg needs to have plenty of dollars on hand, so they tend to export a lot of their trade to the US. Similarly for euro pegs where the nation exports mainly to the Eurozone.

Because the dollar and euro float, it's hard to keep the pegs exact. Many countries use a price range instead. China pegs to a range for the US dollar and tries to keep its currency low, which makes its exports attractive to the US market.

Therefore, when you want to purchase something in a different country, you need to take the exchange rate into account. Not only that, but you'll likely need the local currency to affect the transaction. If you're an American who wants to buy a place in Italy for your retirement, you'll need to come up with the amount necessary in euros. The dollar is (usually) not worth the same amount in Britain as it is in Italy, because the pound/dollar exchange rate is completely different from the euro/dollar rate, and those are both different from the pound/euro rate as well.

Even though that seems hard enough, those 3 are highly traded currencies so the exchange rate is pretty reasonable. Now imagine that you live in an undeveloped country and your currency is thinly traded (there's not much demand for it). If you want to exchange for another currency, the price will be higher because the demand is low. Seems expensive, right? Don't forget that every time you exchange the currency, you have to pay the intermediary who does the exchange for you separately! You can see why a global currency or global coin is so attractive: a crypto token (such as Bitcoin) is worth the same in Italy as it is in Zimbabwe as it is in the US, no matter what each country's currencies or economies are doing.

Customizable User Experience

When you're in the traditional financial system, you deal with whatever software that particular institution has chosen to use. If your banking interface is hard to understand and use, that's just too bad—your life is harder than it needs to be through no fault of your own.

Of course, it helps if you have some tech knowledge! Or a techie friend who can be enlisted in your quest. You'll be able to browse DApps through your mobile wallet, so you might also find something you like elsewhere and use that instead. As more and more users come to DeFi, designers are beginning to focus on ease of use and intuitiveness in their apps.

Technology does tend to expect that the early adopters have some knowledge. As applications and systems become more mainstream and more non-techies need to use them, the apps become much friendlier to all users.

CHAPERT 8:

Smart Contracts

O ne of the major innovations in decentralized finance is the ability to create smart contracts. Instead of going through lawyers to devise and implement contracts, blockchain allows computers to do it automatically. Having the code responsible for specifying who does what reduces a lot of friction in transactions, which results in—you guessed it—lower costs.

These are Ethereum accounts that can hold money and send it out, or refund it, based on the conditions programmed into the contract. You could have a smart contract that puts a certain amount of money into your child's wallet each month while they're away at college. No additional distributees can be added in since blocks are so difficult to tamper with. Banks can get hacked, but your kid's money is safe. At least until they hit the ATM, anyway.

Your child doesn't have to wait until your check "clears" to access the money, which can take days depending on the traditional bank. On the blockchain, as soon as it's executed, the funds are in their wallet. There's no human intervention required to make it happen, nor can a bank employee being away on vacation affect the deposit.

Because the contracts are open source, they can be audited and viewed so bad contracts are spotted quickly. Remember, the accounts are pseudonymous, so no one knows that it's you sending money to your kid. Miners and nodes only see transactions between two accounts.

As long as the parameters specified in the code of the contract are met, the transaction will be executed. It's common to require a fee for performing the transaction. On Ethereum, the transaction fees are paid in ether tokens, which are commonly referred to as "gas" (Levi et al, 2018).1 At the moment most of the smart contracts are relatively simple in terms of the number of steps the logic of the code asks for. The more complexity, the more "gas" is needed to make it happen.

Technology is great... when it works.

Decentralized finance does share a characteristic with traditional finance: there is no free lunch. There are always trade-offs. DeFi isn't a magic bullet that fixes all the problems with conventional finance. While it's true that computer code can execute flawlessly over and over again when it's written correctly, the fact that it's written by humans means there's still plenty of room for error.

Developers still have to issue bug fixes for their DApps, just as they do for other applications. Back in the 1980s, programmers were trained to remember GIGO: Garbage In, Garbage Out. It's still true whether the code is written on the blockchain or not.

Another issue with smart contracts is that most of them are not particularly legible to non-programmers. Many people get the help of a trained lawyer when they're dealing with a complicated contract (such as a mortgage loan, house purchase, even an agent's agreement) to get the "legalese" translated into ordinary English.

However, even non-lawyers can usually understand very simple contracts, like the one you might sign to set up an automatic distribution from one bank account to another. Even simple smart contracts aren't readily accessible to non-tech people. Anyone entering into a smart contract now either needs to have their own expertise or to hire a programmer to explain the contract to them.

Over time, it's likely that the smart contracts will be easier to read so you don't have to have a programming expert by your side, but we're not quite there yet.

Many smart contracts require input from entities that are not on the blockchain. The blockchain can't pull this information from off-chain resources. The data has to be pushed to it, which can cause mismatches between nodes.

Suppose that a crop insurance smart contract pays the owner a certain amount any time the temperature drops below freezing (32 degrees Fahrenheit). As anyone who lives in the contiguous 48 knows, temperatures can fluctuate wildly from minute to minute. Nodes may receive the information at different times, which could cause one node to reject the block because it received the temperature as 33 degrees instead.

One solution that's been proposed for this type of problem is a predefined, third-party oracle that pulls the relevant information and pushes it to the nodes at certain times. While it's certainly a workable solution, it introduces an intermediary into the equation, which is exactly what the blockchain is designed to prevent.

The oracle may also be a point of failure for the whole system. It might not push the information to the blockchain when necessary, provide wrong data, or even go out of business. An oracle could be hacked, which could compromise the security of the whole blockchain.

A smart contract is a programmable contract that allows two parties to agree on transaction parameters without relying on a third party to carry out the transaction. For example, if Alice wishes to create a trust fund that will pay Bob $100 per month for the next 12 months, she may design a smart contract to do the following: 1. Verify the current date. 2. Send Bob $100 automatically at the beginning of each month 3. Repeat until the smart contract's fund is depleted. Alice has eliminated the requirement for a trusted third-party intermediary (lawyers, escrow agents, etc.) to transfer the trust money to Bob by utilizing a smart contract, and the process has been made visible to all parties involved.

Aside from creating DApps, Ethereum can also be used to create Decentralized Autonomous Organizations (DAO) and issue other cryptocurrencies. A Decentralized Autonomous Organization (DAO) is a completely autonomous organization controlled by code rather than a single person. Based on smart contracts, this code allows DAOs to replace the way traditional organizations are typically run. Because it is based on code, it is immune to human intervention and operates transparently. Any outside influence would have no effect. DAO token voting would be used to make governance decisions or rulings.

In terms of tokens, Ethereum can be used as a platform for the creation of other cryptocurrencies. On the Ethereum Network, there are currently two popular protocols for tokens: ERC-20 and ERC-721. ERC-20 is a protocol standard for the issuing of Ethereum tokens that specifies the rules and criteria. ERC-20 tokens are fungible, which means they can be exchanged for one another and have the same value. ERC-721 tokens, on the other hand, are non-fungible, which means they are unique and cannot be exchanged. Consider ERC-20 to be money and ERC-721 to be collectibles such as action figures or baseball cards.

Role of Smart Contracts in DeFi

As the DeFi sector has grown from a small industry in 2018 to one of the fast-developing industries in the digital technology world, the usage of smart contracts has accelerated in 2020.

Many cryptocurrencies and decentralized applications (DApps) work using smart contract code to support the trading of products, services, data, funds, *etc.* While users of the centralized financial sector, like banks or credit institutions, can depend on third parties to handle a transaction. DApps need to use smart contracts to make sure that every transaction is valid, transparent, and trustless—and that products or services are being transferred in line with the predefined provisions of the agreement.

In summary, smart contracts make sure that the parties in an agreement are both fulfilling their part of the agreement.

Advantages of Utilizing Smart Contracts

Smart contracts have many advantages over traditional centralized applications or agreements. Smart contracts are more effective than conventional centralized ways of trading products, services, or information because they are quicker, more open, precise, and stable. Users do not have to trust a centralized system's blackbox; instead, they can rely on "code is law" to precisely see how each application behaves.

These efficiencies combine to create a much more cost-effective method of handling the trading of commodities, products, and services.

Problems with DeFi and Smart Contracts

There are some possible issues to remember when used in a DeFi setting. Smart contracts in a decentralized system access external data that must be checked in some other way in the absence of a centralized, authenticated data source.

DeFi users, for instance, need accurate price feeds to ensure that the value of a digital asset is valid and devoid of external manipulation, allowing them to transact securely and efficiently in a decentralized environment.

Using a data-oracle platform, like Band Protocol, as a remedy to this problem. By giving access to trusted, authenticated data from different sources, data oracle platforms enable decentralized applications to profit from smart contracts. Smart contracts can then be performed without the need for external intervention and remain completely decentralized.

Future of Smart Contract

The acceptance possibility of smart contract features is hard to comprehend since there is no limit. Smart contracts can change many processes across a wide range of sectors, eliminating administrative delays and developing robust self-executing systems.

There are several existing use cases for smart contracts in use all over the world, for example. Here are some of them:

- **Peer-to-peer payments and transactions**. Trusted third parties, or intermediaries, such as financial institutions and agents, are no longer needed with distributed ledger technology (DLT). Smart contracts take all the permissions and procedures that these conventional players used to do. It can also accelerate the transaction, but the high speed of traditional financial networks cannot presently be surpassed due to the logistics of proving transaction validity.
- **Digital identity.** The importance of each human being having a distinct identity has made the headline recently.

Instead of issuing identification cards or physical passports, the only feasible way to provide anyone with an ID in the shortest amount of time is to use a digital ID. This is why digital identity is such an essential part of DeFi.

- **Digital marketplaces.** One of the most common DeFi use cases is creating marketplaces that connect buyers and sellers, depending on smart contracts to allow direct trading without the need for a third party or a broker. The market's reach is very broad, ranging from community-based, regional markets that help SMEs by providing buyers with tokens to buy local to markets that offer sellers access to international markets without having to deal with brokerage firms like Amazon eBay. Collectors and investors may also participate in niche markets, such as those in the art world.

- **Tokenization.** The significance of blockchain as a network has been acknowledged as the network matures. Initially, blockchain was all about bitcoin. However, as the network grows, the significance of blockchain as a platform has been acknowledged. Tokens have advantages beyond their use as a medium of exchange:

    o **They are fractional.** With Bitcoin's current value hovering about $23,000, a single coin is out of reach for many potential investors. Anyone, though, can buy a few Satoshis, or one hundred millionth of a Bitcoin. The nature of the token and the function it serves can be customized to meet the needs of the market. Rather than targeting conventional lenders and markets, a business will use an Initial Coin Offering to raise funds.

○ **There are still risks associated with cryptos, especially the market's uncertainty**. This has resulted in creating tokens such as stablecoins, which are connected to major currencies like dollars or euros and provide market stability.

Risk of Smart Contract

Although the future of blockchain appears positive, and many existing economic systems are expected to switch to the blockchain in the near future, it is still a young sector. At first glance, DeFi appears to be a fantastic way to launch a new financial product quickly, but a thorough knowledge of the risks associated with smart contracts is essential.

This may involve the following:

- Wrong contract structuring due to inaccuracies in coding and specifications.
- Inadequate cybersecurity defense to defend against hacking.

- Legislative changes. Many governments are still figuring out how to regulate the cryptocurrency industry, and improvements to the contract structure can be made.

- Contracts are being used inefficiently, resulting in unnecessary costs. Although Ethereum isn't the only network that supports DeFi, it controls 80% of the marketplace. Smart contracts include "gas," which must be paid any time a contract is executed. This can lead to unexpected costs, making the DeFi application unprofitable and therefore unappealing to potential customers.

- The role of smart contract audit in reducing these possible risks is now recognized by most entities that have already deployed blockchain solutions. Smart contract auditors assist in the optimization of smart contracts and the detection of threats and inconsistencies in the code.

- People and institutions are rapidly transforming how they share information, receive financial services, and communicate with one another thanks to smart contracts. We hope to see smart contracts deployed broadly across all conventional business sectors in due time as distributed ledger technology keeps making our online platforms more accessible and effective.

CHAPERT 9:

The Digital Wallet

A wallet is a software that stores private and public keys. It communicates with different blockchains to allow people to send and receive digital currency while also keeping track of their balance. You'll need a digital wallet if you wish to use Bitcoin or some other crypto.

Digital wallets are used by millions of individuals, although there is a lot of confusion about how they work. Digital wallets, unlike conventional "pocket" wallets, do not store currency. In reality, currencies do not exist in any physical form and are not stored in any location. The only thing that remains is transaction details stored on blockchain technology.

Digital wallets are computer programs that store your public and private keys and connect to blockchain networks so you can check your balance, transfer money, and do other things. When someone sends you Ethereum or some other form of cryptocurrency, they effectively sign off on the coins' rights to your wallet's address. The private key held in your wallet should match the public address the coin is allocated to spend certain coins and access the funds. The balance in your digital wallet will rise if the public and private keys match, and the senders will reduce correspondingly. There is no physical exchange of money. A transaction record on the network and a change in balance in your crypto wallet are all needed to complete the transaction.

Non-Custodial vs. Custodial

Custodial and non-custodial wallets are the 2 types of wallets. Custodial wallets are those in which intermediaries hold and manage your cryptos on your behalf. Non-custodial wallets offer you complete total control and the right to your cryptos. This is close to the mantra of many individuals in the blockchain market's "be your bank."

When you use a custodial wallet, you're putting your confidence in a third party to secure your coins. This can be advantageous because you will not have to stress about protecting your private key; instead, you would have to care about the vulnerability of your account details, similar to how you might secure your email account. Although, entrusting your cryptos to a third party exposes you to the possibility of the custodian losing your cryptos due to poor management or hacking. Custodial wallets have been known to lose their cryptos in the past, with Mt. Gox being the most well-known example. In 2014, Mt. Gox lost over 850,000 bitcoin worth over $450 million.

When you use a non-custodial wallet, you are relying solely on yourself to keep your cryptos secure. Nevertheless, when using a non-custodial wallet, you transfer the security responsibility to yourself, and you must be completely prepared to store your private keys securely. You will lose access to your cryptos if you lose your private keys.

There is an ever-expanding list of possibilities. Nevertheless, before you choose a wallet, think about how you want to use it.

- Do you really need a digital wallet for daily transactions, or simply want to invest in cryptocurrency and keep it in your wallet?
- Do you want to use multiple currencies or only one?
- Do you want to be able to reach your crypto wallet from anywhere or only at home?

Take some time to consider your needs before deciding on the best wallet for you. There are a plethora of digital wallets in the market. We'll show you how to use a few of the DeFi-friendly wallets to get started with the DeFi network for this book.

1. Argent

Argent wallet is a good choice for smartphone users. Argent is a non-custodial wallet that combines ease of use with high security, which isn't always the case. It does so by using Argent

Guardians, individuals, computers, or third-party providers who can confirm your identity.

Family and friends that use Argent, other hardware or Metamask wallets, or two-factor authentication services are all examples. Argent is reconsidering the need for paper-based seed phrase backups while restoring accounts using this small circle of the trusted network.

If your wallet is stolen, Argent Guardians enable you to lock it and immediately freeze all funds. After five days, your wallet will be automatically unlocked, or you can ask your Argent Guardian to unlock it earlier.

You can also add extra security features to your wallet, like a daily transaction cap, to make it safer. This helps stop hackers from stealing money from your Argent wallet if they obtain access to it. When your daily transaction cap is reached, you will be notified, and any transactions that exceed the limit will be delayed for more than 24 hours. You may, of course, use your Argent Guardians to sanction valid large transactions that exceed the cap.

Argent provides wallet users with free transactions and removes all Ethereum gas fees that must be charged to the network. You can communicate with DeFi DApps easily from the Argent wallet, eliminating the need for another app or gadget.

There is presently a waiting list to use the Argent wallet. You may sign up using this link (non-sponsored) to bypass the queue: https://argent.link/coingecko.

Argent Step-by-Step Guide

- **Step 1.** Go to https://argent.link/coingecko. Install the app on your smartphone.
- **Step 2.** Develop a unique name for your argent wallet once it has been installed.
- **Step 3.** Argent will ask you if you like to add your phone number for additional protection and authentication.
- **Step 4.** Argent will then request your email address for verification purposes.
- **Step 5.** You will be put on a waiting list. You may sign up using this link to bypass the queue: https://argent.link/coingecko. When your wallet is available for use, you will receive an email update.
- **Step 6.** You begin to deposit or transfer cryptos to others. To boost your security, try adding more Argent Guardians.

2. Metamask

Metamask, a web browser feature available for Chrome, Firefox, Opera, and Brave, is a good option for desktop users. Metamask, similar to Argent, is a non-custodial wallet that serves as both a wallet and an Ethereum platform interaction bridge.

Metamask is where you can keep your Ethereum and ERC20 tokens. Metamask acts as an interaction bridge, allowing you to use all Ethereum Network-hosted Decentralized Applications (DApps).

Suppose you were operating a complete Ethereum node and had the whole Ethereum blockchain of over 400GB loaded on your server. In that case, your browser will not be able to access the Ethereum network without using an interaction bridge-like MetaMask. On a technical level, MetaMask accomplishes this by inserting web3.js, a JavaScript library created by the Ethereum core developers, into your browser's tab, allowing you to communicate with the Ethereum platform with ease.

On your laptop or PC, Metamask makes interacting with DeFi DApps on the Ethereum platform a breeze. They are safe to some extent since each connection and transaction you perform on the network must be signed.

To ensure your Metamask is safe and stable, you should take precautions. Anyone who knows your password or seed phrase (a hidden phrase you were given when you signed up for your wallet) has full power over your wallet. Metamask can be used to access many DeFi DApps.

Metamask Step-by-Step Guide

- **Step 1.** Go to https://metamask.io/. Install an extension for your preferred browser.

- **Step 2.** Click "Get Started" after you've loaded the extension.

- **Step 3.** Select "Create a Wallet" and click "Next."

- **Step 4.** Create a password.

- **Step 5.** (This is really critical! Read carefully!) A secret backup phrase will be issued to you. Do not lose it. It should never be shown to anybody. You won't be able to recover the phrase if you lose it. Anyone who has it has access to your wallet and can do anything they want with it.

- **Step 6.** You will be asked to write it to ensure that you have written down the provided hidden backup phrase.

- **Step 7.** Congratulations on your achievement! Your wallet has been created! It can now be used to store Ethereum and ERC20 tokens.

- **Step 8.** Your wallet's public key or Ethereum address will be displayed. If anyone wishes to give you coins, they will scan your QR code.

3. Burner Wallet

The Burner Wallet began as a basic web application: a digital wallet with a QR code scanner with a send form. The Ether community develops a slew of ideas for future burner wallet functionality as the project's popularity rose.

The Burner Wallet has proven to be a helpful platform for rookies to cryptos and blockchain networks.

CHAPERT 10:

DeFi Marketplaces

There are no intermediaries in a decentralized marketplace. The idea is somewhat close to how a traditional blockchain works.

You install the client program on your computer. When you run it, it will immediately bind you to anyone else who is running the software. You will eliminate the need for any intermediaries in this manner.

Though OpenBazaar is based on Ricardian smart contracts, Ethereum is used by the majority of decentralized marketplaces. It's easy to see why Ethereum is the industry leader in crypto marketplaces, just as it is with DeFi. For starters, it has the first-mover benefit thanks to its groundbreaking smart contract platform. Finally, they have the most sought-after and well-regarded developer culture in the sector.

The biggest problem with Ethereum right now is its lack of scalability. Ethereum has a transaction rate of just 15 transactions per second.

You'll need a quicker and more stable network if you desire an efficient marketplace. As a result, developers have begun experimenting with blockchain networks. What platform you choose is determined by what you're looking for.

OpenBazaar

OpenBazaar is a peer-to-peer (P2P) marketplace that links buyers and sellers. The following factors have contributed to OpenBazaar's high visibility:

- Its graphical user interface (GUI) is extremely user-friendly and straightforward.
- The marketplace program is easy to use. After you've installed the software, you're ready to go.
- Finally, there are several types of assets available for exchange in the marketplace.

Data sharing/tracking is an option in OpenBazaar. If you choose not to do so, your data will be protected.

You can also transact with Zcash, a privacy coin, to keep your transaction information private. No single entity regulates OpenBazaar. In a peer-to-peer network, all nodes contribute nearly equally to the platform.

Bitcoin, Bitcoin Cash, Litecoin, and Zcash are among the more than 50 cryptos accepted by OpenBazaar.

Mode of Payment on OpenBazaar

OpenBazaar makes use of Bitcoin's Escrow function to render the payment structure as secure as possible. Here's what you should remember about this feature:

- Before beginning a transaction, buyers and sellers should settle on a trusted third party.
- The buyer sends their preferred crypto and has it kept in escrow.
- Only when a minimum of two of the 3 parties consents on the legality of the transaction are the funds issued.

There are 3 types to be aware of when it comes to payments: direct, moderated, and offline.

- **Direct Payments.** When both entities are online, the buyer immediately sends crypto to the seller in this network. This is a simple transaction with few complexities.
- **Moderated Payments.** This method of payment works as follows:
  - As a moderator, the buyer selects an intermediary.
  - The fund is deposited in an escrow account. When financing this escrow, the buyer pays a fee.
  - The seller pays a fee as the assets leave the escrow.

It's important to remember that these payments will only be possible if two out of 3 parties agree. If neither the buyer nor the seller is ready, they will have to deal with the moderator. If the moderator is interested, nevertheless, they may also charge a fee.

- **Offline Payments.** Suppose the buyer intends to pay an offline seller directly. In that case, the assets are placed in a provisional escrow account. Both the buyer and the seller can communicate at any moment. Whatever the case may be, the seller now has the following options:
  - They go online and have the option of accepting or rejecting the bid. The sellers will collect the funds minus a fee if they approve the order.
  - If the seller never responds to the bid or refuses it, the buyer returns the escrow assets and pays a fee.

OpenSea Marketplace

OpenSea is a blockchain platform for cryptocurrency products such as collectibles and game pieces that runs on Ethereum. Buyers and sellers will communicate with one another directly through smart contracts on this network. The firm was established in 2018 by Alex Atallah and Devin Finzer. The co-founders have remarkable histories with Palantir, Google, Facebook, and other companies.

What You Can Achieve With OpenSea

OpenSea is best known for trading non-fungible tokens or NFTs. What exactly do we mean by "non-fungible"?

In simple terms, this simply means that each token is one-of-a-kind. Do you recall cryptokitties?

Those collectible, virtual cats that once flooded the Ethereum platform?

They are probably the most popular example of NFTs.

How OpenSea Works

OpenSea is very easy to use and understand. Simply follow the steps below:

The first step is to plug in your Metamask. The OpenSea app looks through your wallet for any collectibles you may have. It will equally tell you the cryptocurrency you'll need to purchase products on the market.

If you've logged in, you'll have 2 options: buy a product or sell a product. Users may offer an offer if the seller has a fixed price or acknowledge the list price if the seller has not.

Listing is free. If the product is successfully sold, OpenSea charges a small fee of 2.5% of the final amount.

Particl Marketplace

If OpenBazaar is the "O.G." decentralized marketplace and OpenSea is the Ethereum-based option, Particl is the outlier keeping its own in the space. Ryno Mathee founded Particl with the aim of creating a decentralized, P2P, and completely anonymous cryptocurrency marketplace. The native token of Particl is PART. It's a version of ShadowProject (SDC), which was a privacy coin at the time. Particl's decentralized marketplace is the most essential feature behind its growing popularity. The alpha version of the stable peer-to-peer platform was released in 2018. The following are some of the marketplace's properties:

- The user data is not stored on a server and is not exchanged with anybody else.
- All transactions are confidential and anonymous.
- The market makes sure that the system is fully decentralized and trustworthy.
- Apart from that, Particl is also relatively easy to use.
- The desktop client is simple to download and set up.
- Once you've installed it, you'll need to build a wallet inside this market to make all of your transactions.
- Particl allows merchants to maximize their profit margins by up to 40%.
- Particl's native token is PART.

The following are some things to keep in mind about the PART token:

- PART purchases are completely anonymous and confidential.
- It's compatible with the atomic swap. This implies it can switch from one user to another without requiring an exchange.
- By using cryptographic strategies such as Ring CT, PART guarantees confidentiality.

CHAPERT 11:

DeFi Platform for Investing

Terra Luna

I t is a blockchain protocol that uses fiat-linked stablecoins like TerraUSD to create global payment systems. It has two cryptocurrencies, the LUNA token is used in the form of collateral to achieve stablecoin price stability.

The process that this currency uses is similar to that of DAI but done in reverse. While with DAI you must collateralize the loan by creating a new DAI, in Terra you must burn LUNA tokens. DAI expands the monetary base and LUNA reduces it. To create new USTs, you have to burn the equivalent dollar amount of LUNA.

Imagine that LUNA is worth 10 euros, a person has 10, he would then have 100 euros and the price of the stablecoin UST is above one euro. In this case, those who have LUNA would want to burn them to create UST and earn. For example, the UST is €1.30, by burning them, they would have 30% profit. 130 euros.

The balance between Terra and Luna makes an analogy of the earth and the moon, the latter is responsible for ordering the tides and marking the rhythm and stability on earth.

Uniswap

It is one of the best known in the blockchain world. It has become one of the biggest DEX in the crypto ecosystem. Uniswap is one of the biggest contenders for centralized solutions that allow you to exchange cryptocurrencies using smart contracts over the Ethereum network.

Uniswap works with the ERC-20 ether token. It has its limitations, such as not being able to exchange with other cryptos, although there are other ERC-20 tokens anchored 1:1. Thus they can be exchanged for other cryptocurrencies. This allows other opportunities to be taken advantage of and that is why this DeFi has not stopped growing since its birth.

Uniswap is more than just a DEX, it was created as an AMM protocol, which means that it is able to allow users to create markets from which third parties can benefit. The creation of these markets is self-sustaining, allowing the protocol to generate revenue to incentivize the injection of liquidity in exchange for a small interest to its investors.

Chainlink (Link)

It has its own token that is exchanged on the same platform and that you can also buy on major exchanges. The main function is to connect the blockchain network with the off-chain system. It was the first middleware created to securely monitor payments, market data, and financial systems such as web applications, APIs, PayPal, and bank accounts with Bitcoin, Ethereum, and HyperLedger smart contracts.

Chainlink is based on a network of nodes called Chainlink Nodes. The function is that it feeds smart contracts running on Ethereum with data taken from one or more real-world events. In addition, it uses incentive policy as a data protection measure. This prevents malicious manipulations or malpractices with the data obtained. In this way, it establishes financial compensation, as an incentive for correct answers of node operators.

Fantom

It was created in mid-2018, it aims to create a platform of smart contracts characterized by fast and cheap transactions, its goal is to be competitive with Ethereum. The cryptocurrency uses the technology known as Directed Acyclic Graph (DAG), by means DAG can be freed from the restrictions implied by the existence of predefined block sizes, increasing the speed of predefined block sizes, increasing the speed of execution, and reducing the number of network confirmations.

The creators of Fantom wanted to use the system to build infrastructure to develop what are known as smart cities. The creators know the potential of DeFi, so they have incorporated the ability to issue synthetic assets as well as trade them and make loans from any Fantom wallet.

Tezos

This cryptocurrency burst into the crypto space collecting $232 million. Its official launch was in 2018. It is a new decentralized blockchain that governs itself through the establishment of a true Digital Commonwealth.

Its goal is to get token owners to work together to make decisions that improve the protocol over time. It was developed by Arthur Breitman, who studied applied mathematics, computer science and physics in France and later moved to the United States. Although it has been a crypto with many complexities, it has been preferred by many for investment.

Aave

It is a decentralized lending platform that has become a big and important project in the industry. It works on the Ethereum blockchain and was originally known as ETHLend. It was dedicated to allowing users to put cryptocurrencies at the service of third parties, making loans. Its service was very simple because there were two modalities:

- A lender opens a loan position under certain conditions and it was listed on the platform. Interested users could view the offers and accept the one they were interested in.
- A user could make a loan request that could be fulfilled by a lender if he accepted the conditions stipulated in the request.

In the beginning, the platform worked with ETH and a few ERC-20 but the diversity of tokens has increased having stablecoins like USDT and DAI, using cryptocurrencies like Bitcoin which makes it flexible in this aspect.

DOT

It is a cryptocurrency that runs within the Polkadot chain. This proposal integrates all cryptocurrencies so that different blocks can make transactions with each other. Its plan is to revolutionize the market by making it more efficient and economical every day. The main feature is the creation of bridges to generate parachains. This cryptocurrency has a lot of potentials and is growing daily, promising to be a very juicy source of investment in both the short and long term.

ADA

This is the cryptocurrency that runs on the Cardano blockchain. It has the proposal to execute smart contracts, develop self-interest projects instead of just transacting cryptos. It allows interoperability between blockchains.

The network has a goal to bring the third generation of cryptocurrencies and in 2021 alone it has appreciated 982%. Despite this, ADA goes up and down like all cryptocurrencies, corrections happen frequently.

In addition, Cardano will launch a new stablecoin DeFi in partnership with Coti.

SOL

It is the token born from the Solana blockchain. It was released in 2019 and managed to scale DeFi's products and protocols. Solana's initial proposal was to perform 50 thousand transactions per second, but it reached 400000 TPS when the network collapsed.

In comparison, Bitcoin performs 7 transactions per second and Ethereum up to 25 TPS. Grayscale recently added SOL and UNI to the Digital Large Cap Fund portfolio.

Chilliz

This is a token that aims to decentralize and tokenize the sports media. It has an international debit card with cashback benefits. The more it grows the more the fans will talk about it and the more the price will go up. The opposite can also happen, for example, if fans and teams don't make much use of it, the price can drop.

This is a cryptocurrency that has risen considerably and can cause big changes in the sports world.

CAKE

This is the decentralized exchange PancakeSwap that trades cryptocurrency projects. It allows users to trade tokens and generate passive income. It has great upside advantages. To date, it has had an increase of more than 4000%.

It is among the cryptocurrencies that can have a high valuation.

Maker

This is a platform that sells DAI tokens and seeks to reduce volatility. The DAI token is exchanged at a value of one dollar, which highlights stability with several variants, such as external market mechanisms and economic incentives.

Dai is on the verge of being the most stable cryptocurrency.

Maker was the first token on the Ethereum network and then on the Maker platform. It was launched in 2016. Before the platform was released, funds were issued through the exchange of Bitcoins and Ethereum for MKR tokens. In December 2017, the Maker network took a step forward, created a dollar-linked asset with a one-for-one exchange rate.

In order to access the Maker system, a CDP is generated. When the debt is paid, the user has control over Dai. The same happens when a customer converts Ethereum coins to Pooled Ether.

CHAPERT 12:

DeFi Derivatives

A derivative contract derives its value from another underlying asset, such as stocks, commodities, currencies, indices, bonds, or interest rates. Futures, options, and swaps are some examples of derivatives. Each sort of derivative serves a particular purpose, and investors buy and sell them for various reasons.

Investors trade derivatives for various purposes, including hedging against the underlying asset's volatility, speculating on the directional movement of the underlying asset and leveraging their holdings. Derivatives are extremely dangerous, and trading them requires extensive financial expertise and methods.

DeFi derivatives DApps have a total value of $114.3 million, representing 12% of the DeFi ecosystem. Though the figure is low compared to other DeFi markets, such as lending ($745.6 million), it is worth considering that the decentralized derivative market has only been active for one year and has grown rapidly. Synthetix and bZx are two important DeFi derivative Protocols.

Synthetix

Synthetix is, as the name implies, a protocol for Ethereum-based Synthetic Assets (called Synths). Synthetix is made up of two parts: Synthetic Assets (Synths) and its exchange, Synthetix. Exchange. Synthetix enables the creation and exchange of Synths.

Synths are assets or a combination of assets with the same value or impact as another item. Synths follow the value of underlying assets and provide exposure to them without requiring the actual asset to be held.

Normal Synths and Inverse Synths are the two types of Synths currently available. Normal Synths are positively connected with the underlying assets, whereas Inverse Synths are adversely correlated.

Synthetic Gold (sXAU) is an example of a Synthetic Asset because it tracks the price performance of gold. Synthetix tracks real-world asset values using Chainlink, a smart contract oracle that collects price information from various trusted third-party sources to prevent tampering.

Inverse Bitcoin (iBTC) is an example of an Inverse Synthetic Asset since it follows the inverse price performance of Bitcoin. Each Inverse Synths has 3 critical values: the entry price, the lower limit, and the higher limit.

As an example, consider Inverse Synthetic Bitcoin (iBTC). Assume that Bitcoin (BTC) is priced at $10,600 at the time of formation—this will be the entrance price. If Bitcoin falls from $400 to $10,200, the iBTC Synth will be worth $400 more and will be priced at $11,000. The inverse will also be true. If Bitcoin reaches $11,000, the iBTC Synth is now worth $10,200.

Inverse Synths trade in a range that has a 50% upper and lower limit from the entering price. This limits the maximum profit or loss you can make on Inverse Synths. When any of the limits is reached, the exchange rates for the tokens are frozen, and the positions are liquidated. These Inverse Synths can only be swapped at Synthetix once they have been disabled and liquidated. At those predetermined values, you can exchange. They are then reset with new limitations.

As previously said, Synths provide traders with price exposure to the asset without the requirement to possess the underlying asset. Synthetic Gold (sXAU) allows traders to engage in the market with far less bother than regular gold brokerages (no sign-ups, no traveling, no middleman, etc.).

Another advantage of synthetics is that they may be traded without friction, which means that Synthetic Gold can be readily exchanged for Synthetic JPY, Synthetic Silver, or Synthetic Bitcoin on Synthetix.Exchange. This also implies that anyone having an Ethereum wallet now has unrestricted access to any real-world asset!

The concept of creating Synths is similar to that of creating DAI on Maker. Before you can construct DAI based on the collateral submitted, you must first stake ETH as collateral on Maker's smart contract. For Synths, you must first invest in the Synthetix Network Token (SNX), which serves as the system's collateral. SNX is less liquid than ETH, and its price is more erratic overall. To compensate, a significant minimum initial collateral of 750% is required on Synthetic, compared to minimum initial collateral of 150% on Maker. This means that to mint $100 in Synthetic USD (sUSD), you'll need at least $750 in SNX as collateral.

Synth minting is a rather complex system. It entails the staker incurring debt, the levels of which are dynamically modified based on the overall value of Synths in the global debt pool, leading the staker's debt to fluctuate with changing prices. For example, if all Synths in the system were synthetic Ethereum (sETH) and the price doubled, everyone's debt, including the staker's debt, would quadruple.

Index Synths

Index Synths is one of the more fascinating Synths accessible on Synthetix. At the time of writing, there are two Index Synths: sCEX and sDEFI. Index Synths give traders exposure to a basket of tokens without requiring them to buy all of them. The performance of the underlying tokens will be reflected in the index. Index Synths provide exposure to specific parts of the business and risk diversification without the need to hold and manage several tokens.

sCEX

sCEX is an Index Synth aimed to provide traders with exposure to a basket of Centralized Exchange (CEX) tokens with a weighted market capitalization that approximates their weighted market capitalization. The sCEX index presently includes Binance Coin (BNB), Bitfinex's LEO Token (LEO), Huobi Token (HT), OKEx Token (OKB), and KuCoin Shares (KCS).

There is also the iCEX Inverse Synth, which is the inverse of the sCEX Index Synth and works similarly to other Inverse Synths.

Synthetix Exchange

Exchange is a decentralized exchange platform built for exchanging SNX and Synths without the use of order books that most DEXs use. Unlike a peer-to-peer system (Uniswap or dYdX), Synthetix does not rely on users to supply liquidity. Users can trade directly against a contract with appropriate constant liquidity, theoretically reducing the risk of slippage or lack of liquidity.

Users can buy up to the complete amount of collateral in the system without affecting the contract's price because they purchase a synthetic contract rather than trading the underlying asset. A $10,000,000 BTC buy/sell order, for example, would almost certainly result in significant slippage on traditional exchanges, but not on Synthetix Exchange because customers trade directly against the Synthetix contract.

Another thing to know about Synthetix is that they plan to debut a slew of additional trading tools in 2020, including synthetic indices and stocks, leveraged trading, binary options, synthetic futures, and triggered orders.

CHAPERT 13:

Risk and Challenges

The risk factors below are not meant to be comprehensive; however, they represent key weaknesses in DeFi infrastructure that have been or can be taken advantage of. We expect more sophisticated techniques to be deployed in the future as these platforms continue to blossom.

It is necessary to monitor and analyze positions before entry, during the holding period, and after an exit to maintain a sustainable allocation to DeFi.

Perception Is Reality

For many people, decentralized finance doesn't mean anything. They may have heard of cryptocurrencies in general, and they've probably heard of Bitcoin. Both these terms, however, have a bad reputation with a lot of ordinary people who don't know much about finance or technology.

The reputational problems begin with the original whitepaper published in 2008 that posited an alternative finance solution that avoided financial institutions. The name on the whitepaper is Satoshi Nakamoto, but to this day, it's unclear whether this is an actual person or a group of people. This is unfortunate because creating peer-to-peer alternatives is a logical reaction to many of the events leading up to the Great Recession.

Relative Youth

Some of the issues with DeFi are due to the relative infancy of the idea. It was only conceived this century, and we're not very far into the 21st yet. Difficulties such as high price volatility are at least partly a result of the markets still being relatively small. As more people begin to adopt the system, some of that will subside.

It's a bit of a chicken-or-egg dilemma. People don't trust crypto because it fluctuates so much, but it fluctuates so much because not enough people are in the crypto market. These types of growing pains are typical for a lot of technology, especially this century.

It also means that the theory behind the blockchain is only now being practically tested, with the expected results that the original designers didn't consider. Although, in theory, the Mt. Gox theft should have been impossible, it wasn't.

Crypto designers didn't spend enough time considering the security of all the entities that touched Bitcoin. They assumed that the block security protocols and difficulty mining blocks would solve all the problems. They were wrong.

When it comes to money, most of the public wants to know it's safe when they put it somewhere. Having a lot of people lose a lot of value because the designers didn't consider security everywhere they needed is not exactly a recipe for trust.

New tech always has bugs. People are likely to forgive growing pains when those pains happen to a piece of software, not when bugs affect the money that they need to live on. Major financial institutions, central banks, and exchanges spend a lot of money defending against attacks and implementing new security protocols to keep an Mt. Gox from happening to them.

That's a lesson DeFi must learn if it expects to be widely adopted. What are the potential failure points, and how do you protect against them?

Competitive Landscape: Traditional System

You've seen how much a decentralized system with fewer intermediaries can potentially benefit people across the globe by giving them more access to capital without needing a sizable chunk of money, to begin with.

The existing traditional players have a lot of power and they're closely linked with government structures as well. Any alternative that's going to be widely adopted has to be recognized as being just as secure as the existing structure, and DeFi currently is not.

You might think (or hope) that the failure of governments and banking institutions during the Great Recession might have an effect on people who use the current system. After all, only one (foreign) banker in the US went to jail, and none of the others did. In fact, some of the banks that played a big part in the meltdown are stronger than ever.

Depending on your political beliefs, there are easy scapegoats on the "other" side: conservatives blame greedy homeowners and the government for loosening lending standards. Liberals blame the mortgage companies who made bad loans and the banks who packaged the loans. The underlying structure, however, has largely escaped comment, at least among the general public and the media. Most people are not blaming the centralized system for being the culprit.

Not to mention that the existing system already has a lot of political power, in addition to money. Its members regularly lobby the government, and because of their deep pockets, they're the ones to listen to.

Can you buy, for example, Facebook's Libra coin? Recall that it was pulled due to concerns that it would affect the traditional system. If you're considering a cryptocurrency that's usable around the world it's not a bad idea to base it on a basket of currencies, not just the US dollar or euro or yuan.

That's not a terrible business model. Although you can certainly argue that an entity other than a social media company known for privacy invasion should launch it. It was pulled, not because it wouldn't succeed, but because it might succeed too well.

The blockchain will need to figure out a way to work around the power structure coziness to attract more business.

Human Error (Developers)

Tech works really well—when it's working! We've all been at a store when their connection goes down or their automated sales system stops working or had some issue with software, etc. Almost every software release goes out with bugs because the prevailing culture is to just ship it and let the users tell you about the bugs. Again, people are often willing to deal with it when it comes to software but not necessarily when that software is dealing with their money.

There's no guarantee that a developer creating smart contracts can make sure they're bug-free. Things often get missed, even when you're working with open-source code or programs designed to be easily read, like the Go programming language.

Of course, there's no manager to call if the auto-execute feature doesn't work like it was supposed to.

For example, suppose that an investor buys an option contract on a blockchain that is designed to automatically run if the options are in the money at expiration, a bug prevents the program from executing. The user on the other side of the trade might not mind, but that investor will. Who do they go to?

It's not the other side's fault that the 3rd party smart contract didn't work, so they're not going to make the investor whole. Who will? The developer? Will the investor even know who the developer is? Some platforms offer insurance, but what if the users decide they don't want to pay out that claim? That's the kind of uncertainty that investors are not willing to risk money on.

Poor User Experiences

Most blockchain users currently are at least reasonably tech-savvy and can figure out what they need to know or do when presented with an interface that isn't intuitive. Though they may still be annoyed when things are taking too long to wind their way onto a block, or the system is otherwise slow in processing something.

In order for more people to adopt the technology, it has to be friendlier to people who aren't tech-savvy. You've probably heard the howls of outrage every time a social media platform changes the format of something its users like. Even if the GUI is simpler, it still takes time for the public to get used to it and get comfortable with it.

Poor Performance

Blockchain processing can take longer than similar processes in the traditional system, due to the large number of nodes that are involved. Centralized systems don't rely on tens or hundreds of computers scattered around the globe, and their transaction times are therefore usually much faster. While some networks boast of their performance speeds of so many transactions (tx) per second, that's usually in a controlled environment with a much more limited number of nodes than what real-world users experience.

Higher Transaction Costs

Clients (or users) of DeFi do a lot of the computational work through decentralized systems. While the blockchain platforms are faster and lighter, it may take a user's computer some time to actually perform the calculations and get the digital signatures necessary for game or wallet transactions.

The more layers of cryptography (that secure the transactions), the longer it takes. From the user's perspective, it slows them down.

Sustainability

The fact is that the earth is getting warmer due to human activity. The Greenhouse Effect is due to the Earth's atmosphere trapping heat that would otherwise dissipate out into space. Certain gases that have increased due to human activity contribute to the effect, including methane, nitrous oxide (NO), and carbon dioxide (CO2). Burning fossil fuels results in much more NO and CO2, which makes the planet heat up faster. While 3 degrees warmer doesn't seem like it could do much damage, it would cause glaciers to melt and a number of coastal cities would disappear underwater, such as Osaka, Shanghai, Rio de Janeiro, and Miami (Holder et al, 2017). Land that is now used to grow food will no longer support agriculture because the temperatures will be too hot. And so on.

Blockchains that use mining and PoW algorithms use a lot of power, much of which is generated by burning fossil fuels like oil and coal. That's not a sustainable practice, not to mention that many people who are concerned about the environment will refuse to use it. (Remember the artists who pulled back NFTs due to climate concerns.)

Blockchain can actually be a force for good when it comes to the environment. Using it for the supply chain means less waste, and traceability means less fraud and fewer natural resources devoted to fraudulent transactions and products.

The networks, however, have to be PoS and not PoW. What happens to Bitcoin? It's not sustainable. The network has constrained the system to mine only 21 billion coins in total, and as of this writing, slightly less than 19 million have been mined.

Due to the way Bitcoins are structured, it's not expected that the last one will be mined until 2140 (Phillips et al, 2021). By then, unless things change significantly, the earth will be experiencing serious issues with warming as discussed above.

As long as DeFi remains on PoS networks, they won't be contributing to global warming. If Bitcoin doesn't change the way it runs, that might not matter. When catastrophe arrives, it doesn't really matter how we got there.

Printed in Great Britain
by Amazon

78233343R00088